HOW
I PLAY
GOLF

By Tim Williams and Tiger Woods

Dear Dad

Happy Christmas 2001!

lots of love

Tim & Sarah xxx

HOW I PLAY GOLF

BY TIGER WOODS

WITH THE EDITORS OF
GOLF DIGEST

LITTLE, BROWN AND COMPANY

A *Little, Brown* Book

Published simultaneously in Great Britain by
Little, Brown (UK)
and in the United States of America by
Warner Books, Inc., A Time Warner Company
First printing October 2001

A CIP catalogue record for this book is available
from the British Library.

Book design by Judith Turziano

PHOTO CREDITS
Front jacket photograph: Jim Moriarty
Back jacket photograph: Gary Newkirk
Back jacket flap photograph: Stephen Szurlej

All photography by Golf Digest staff photographers
Stephen Szurlej, Dom Furore and Jim Moriarty, unless otherwise noted.
Allsport, Endpaper, VII, 42, 208, 209, 210–211, 212–213, 261, 272–273, 274, 278, 282, 283, 291;
Corbis/Jerry Tubby; Elizabeth Whiting and Associates, 284–285; Bob Ewell, 301–305;
Bill Fields, 77; Rusty Jarrett, 80, 234–235; Larry Lambrecht, 15 (left);
Gary Newkirk, I, 128–129, 142, 206, 226, 227, 244, 257, 267; Larry Petrillo, 276;
Kultida Woods, VIII, 4, 260; Illustrations by Ed Acuña, 28–29, 63, 70, 116, 135, 151, 240–241;
John Corbitt, 12–13, 22, 25, 27, 33, 46, 61, 69, 77, 87, 92, 119, 122, 145, 165,
174, 217, 222–223, 243, 246, 258–259, 265, 266, 286, 288–289 .

Printed and bound in Italy.

Little, Brown & Company (UK)
Brettenham House
Lancaster Place
London WC2E 7EN

To Mom and Pop,

whose love and support

sustain me.

CONTENTS

PREFACE ❖ VIII • FOREWORD ❖ X • ACKNOWLEDGMENTS ❖ XIII

FIRST THINGS FIRST
HOW TO START
YEARNING TO LEARN ❖ 3

THE SHORT GAME
Chapter One
HOW TO PUTT
ROLLING THE ROCK ❖ 21

Chapter Two
HOW TO GET IT DOWN
TURNING THREE INTO TWO ❖ 45

Chapter Three
HOW TO ESCAPE FROM SAND
MAKING THE HARD EASY ❖ 65

THE FULL SWING
Chapter Four
HOW TO SWING
BUILDING AN ACTION TO LAST ❖ 85

Chapter Five
HOW TO FLAG YOUR IRONS
KNOCKING DOWN THE PIN ❖ 115

Chapter Six
HOW TO NAIL FAIRWAY WOODS
PLAYING THE VERSATILE CLUBS ❖ 143

Chapter Seven

HOW TO SMOKE THE DRIVER

GOING WITH ALL YOU'VE GOT ❖ 159

PLAYING THE GAME

Chapter Eight

HOW TO HANDLE PROBLEMS

WHEN IT STARTS GETTING UGLY ❖ 207

Chapter Nine

HOW TO STAY IN CONTROL

MANAGING YOUR GAME ❖ 237

Chapter Ten

HOW TO MASTER THE MIND

WINNING PSYCHOLOGY ❖ 255

FURTHER THOUGHTS

Chapter Eleven

HOW TO GET STRONG

SURVIVING AS THE FITTEST ❖ 275

Chapter Twelve

HOW TO PLAY

ENJOYING THE JOURNEY ❖ 295

AFTERWORD ❖ 306

PREFACE

When Tiger Woods signed an exclusive agreement to write instruction articles for *Golf Digest* in June 1997, there was elation on the part of the editors, and one concern: Was Tiger's knowledge of the golf swing broad and sophisticated enough to convey advice that would help the average golfer improve? Tiger was 21 years old, an age where most players "hit 'em and hunt 'em" without much regard to swing mechanics or strategy. There was no denying his talent as a player—he had won the Masters Tournament just two months previous—but our expectations of Tiger the author/teacher were modest to say the least.

Like the rest of the world, we underestimated Tiger. The first research session with him was a revelation. His grasp of the fundamentals was complete. His understanding of cause and effect in the full swing was astonishing and would grow even richer through time. What's more, his explanations were expansive, articulate and ordered perfectly. He quickly displayed a knack for phrasing his advice in a way that embraced the widest range of golfers possible.

The sum of what Tiger knows about golf is presented in this book. Happily for the reader, Tiger's knowledge has increased over time and extends well beyond his contributions to *Golf Digest*. Tiger's new commitments to physical conditioning, diet, sport psychology and insight into being a tougher competitor are presented here for the first time.

Despite Tiger's eagerness to assist the everyday golfer, the title of this book is *How I Play Golf*. Take note of the "I." Tiger insisted at the outset that he focus on what's right for *him*. Yet, you'll find his methods are sound and far-reaching. When Tiger discourses on the fine points of how he drives the ball 350 yards, you can take comfort knowing that the advice will assist you in your quest for more distance.

At age 25, Tiger has achieved an all-encompassing command of himself, his sport and the world that surrounds it. We hope you enjoy this insight on every facet of the game from the greatest player of his time.

—THE EDITORS OF *GOLF DIGEST*

What a ham: Tiger has been teaching us from the beginning.

FOREWORD

At the 2001 Masters I witnessed Tiger's complete metamorphosis that culminated in a record-setting run of four consecutive major championship victories. His historic accomplishment, inconceivable just two years before, was awesome to behold. Words cannot describe the pleasure and pride I felt when he came into my arms as he walked off the 18th green that Sunday afternoon, the sun sinking behind those huge pine trees. Four years earlier it was a similar scene after Tiger won his initial Masters during his first full year on tour. This time was different. This time I embraced a grown-up who had tried on the title of *best in the world* and found it a perfect fit. I said to him, "You pulled it off. Now you really are in the history books. I love you."

This journey began in the high chair in my garage in Cypress, Calif., where a six-month-old baby watched intently as his father hit balls into a net. Amazingly, he had an attention span of two hours. From the beginning, Tiger had a beautiful, fundamentally sound golf swing. There was just one problem: He was left-handed. It took him two weeks to discover that I was on the other side of the ball. In the middle of a swing, he stopped, walked around on the other side of the ball, changed to a right-handed grip and proceeded to hit the ball into the net perfectly swinging right-handed. I witnessed it and still can't believe it.

His swing developed as he grew older. When Tiger was a teenager it was long, loose and relatively flat. Then he went through a growth spurt and his instructor, John Anselmo, changed his swing plane to more upright to prevent him developing "hookitis" that characterized the early days of Hogan. This swing prevailed through junior and amateur golf. But I knew it had flaws that would have to be corrected. After being eliminated in match play at the 1993 U.S. Amateur at The Champions in Houston, Tiger was reviewed and evaluated by Butch Harmon. Tiger hit a few balls for Butch, who made a startling statement. "Tiger," he said, "Greg Norman had a great pair of hands, but you have the greatest hands I have ever seen." He immediately had Tiger's attention. He then told him, "I'll bet on the downswing, just before impact, you sense whether the club is opened or closed and you make an adjustment with your hands." Tiger said, "Yes, I do." Butch told him they would eliminate that problem by making Tiger's swing plane more consistent to permit the club to come into the hitting area square. Tiger would then be able to use his hands to work the ball. I moved to the edge of the range and watched them work. It was the beginning of a wonderful relationship.

All along, Tiger has been a keen student of the game, displaying tenacity, courage and heart. When he was 8, I told him that he had that extra gear that all great athletes display and that he could call upon it at any time. He knew what I was talking about because we had discussed this while watching players like Magic Johnson, Larry Bird and Kareem Abdul-Jabbar perform their best under pressure. Tiger demonstrated that same ability very early in his development. Setting records at every level of participation, he established a standard of excellence for aspiring golfers. At each level he had the added responsibility of being a minority. Watching him perform under difficult circumstances was inspiring.

Tiger has been a teacher his entire life. I know he has taught me things. The exhibitions he staged for inner-city youth as a teenager have evolved into orchestrated clinics under the auspices of the Tiger Woods Foundation. Just like Tiger, they are competitive in nature, in that each city must submit a proposal to obtain Tiger's services. At his insistence, these clinics are not just ball-striking exhibitions. They present a unique history of the game along with its rules and job opportunities. He is a living example of his family's credo of care and share. I hope this work of love will unlock the door to a wonderful game for those who share in his passion for it. Within its pages you will find wisdom, guidance, technical tips and pure instruction. Listen to Tiger's heart. It is speaking to you. I trust that you will get the message.

—EARL WOODS, *Autumn 2001*

ACKNOWLEDGMENTS

Many thanks to *Golf Digest*

and Warner Books for their collaborative effort

in making this project possible.

Also, grateful acknowledgments to my early teachers

Rudy Duran and John Anselmo, Jay Brunza,

Butch Harmon, who has been my friend and teacher since 1993,

Steve Williams, who has been at my side through many tough rounds

and great moments, writers Pete McDaniel and Guy Yocom,

photographers Dom Furore, Stephen Szurlej and Jim Moriarty,

Golf Digest managing editor Roger Schiffman

and designer Judy Turziano.

FIRST THINGS FIRST

❖ ❖ ❖

Golf is a never-ending journey.

Before we begin, we should

look at where we've been.

HOW TO START

YEARING TO LEARN

I love golf as much for its frankness as for those rare occasions when it rewards a wink with a smile. It is pure, honest and immune to sweet talk. Neither can it be bum-rushed. You must court it slowly and patiently. Any other strategy will be met with a rebuff that for centuries has made grown men and women cry.

Golf does, however, show you moments of vulnerability. They are the reason we relish the courtship and the basis for our hope. It is that flicker of anticipation that draws us from the comfort of ambivalence to the certainty of rejection. Golf does not play favorites. Still we try.

I have been infatuated with the game since my pop first put a club in my hands when I was a toddler. I was an only child, and the club and ball became my playmates. That feeling of solitude and self-reliance enhanced the game's attraction for me and endures today. I suspect that is true of most people who have succumbed to the lure of the game. I recall from conversations with two of the greatest golfers of our time—Arnold Palmer and Jack Nicklaus—that the game had a similar appeal for them. Golf affords you supreme independence. The cliché about the game being you against the golf course is only partly true. Ultimately, it is you against yourself. It always comes down to how well you know yourself, your ability, your limitations and the confidence you have in your ability to execute under pressure that is mostly self-created. Ultimately, you must have the heart and head to play a shot and the courage to accept the consequences.

Golf is a great mirror, often revealing things about you that even you didn't know. It cannot be misled. Still we try.

Sometimes the game comes so easily you can hardly believe it. Every swing seems natural and unforced. Every shot comes off exactly as you envisioned it. That false sense of security is part of the seduction. Every golfer has experienced it. If we are honest with ourselves, we'll admit never quite reaching nirvana—that feeling of invincibility. We are constantly on edge. There is no comfort zone in golf. Nor is it a game of perfection. If it were, we'd all shoot 18 and look for a more challenging sport. I shot a 61—my lowest competitive round—in the third round of the Pac-10 Championships during my sophomore year at Stanford and bogeyed the par-4 14th hole. I actually hit the ball better

YEARNING TO LEARN

3

YOUNG AND (EAGER) RESTLESS

From the beginning I was taught the many facets of golf, that it was much more than just hitting the ball, finding it and hitting it again. It has been a constant learning process with experiences I wouldn't trade for anything. I learned how fundamentals, like never getting the club past parallel on the backswing, were essential for playing the game properly. I also discovered that early success helped boost my confidence and how that translated into a distinct advantage in competition. The trophies were nice, too, but meeting a legend like Sam Snead and getting his autograph were just as cool.

during the afternoon round and shot four strokes worse, including a bogey at 15. Only once do I recall feeling nearly in control of my game and that was when I shot a 13-under-par 59 at my home course in Orlando. Even then I parred both par 5s on the back nine with irons into the greens. The most we can ask of ourselves is to give it our best shot, knowing that sometimes we will fail. We are often defined by how we handle that failure.

The great Ben Hogan, a man not prone to exaggeration, claimed that in his best week of golf he only had four perfect shots. I have yet to get to that higher plane. I won 12 times around the world in 2000, including three majors, and I only remember hitting one shot I would call perfect—a 3-wood

on No. 14 on the Old Course at St. Andrews in the third round of the British Open. From a tight lie I had to hit a little draw into a left-to-right wind and carry the ball about 260 yards to a green guarded by a couple of nasty pot bunkers. As with every shot I attempt, I visualized the ball's flight and how it should respond upon landing. Because it was a blind shot, I picked out a crane in the distance as my target. The ball never left that line and the shot turned out exactly as I had planned. Moments like that stay fresh in my mind, providing a positive image for future reference. Those images are critical when the game is on. They may even be the difference between success and failure.

Sometimes the game seems so difficult you

Reverence for those who helped shape this great game is a responsibility as well as an honor.

I am a naturally
shy person and much
more comfortable on
the golf course than
perhaps anyplace else.
However, winning
makes press conferences
more enjoyable. Some-
times they're even fun.

I can find some creative distractions during those rare times of boredom on the course. This one is good for hand-eye coordination, too.

While I was a student at Stanford University, my putter often gave me sweet success.

wonder whether the effort is worth it. It took me a while to understand why some days you have it and others you don't. Fact is, every day your body feels a little different and golf is such a finite game that a little off can translate into a lot. One or two degrees here and there can mean from four to seven yards. That's not a whole lot but it's magnified due to the precision the game demands. We've all had one of those frustrating days. The final round of the 1996 NCAAs at The Honors Course in Ooltewah, Tenn., was one I'll never forget. I struggled all week, even though I shot some great numbers. I just didn't feel comfortable with my swing. I didn't have the club in the right position, but I was getting away with it because my chipping was great and I made every putt I looked at. I was somehow able to keep the ball in play for most of the holes and let my putter do the rest. In the final round I lost it altogether. I went to the range that morning and never hit a shot. It just

I am never afraid to celebrate my successes and good times with a display of emotion.

Disappointment is part of the game, and how I handle it defines me as a competitor.

wasn't there. Sometimes when that happens you can actually lower your expectations, go out and shoot a great round. Not this time. I played the first three rounds with smoke and mirrors and it finally caught up with me. Fortunately, I had a nine-shot lead and the 80 didn't cost me an individual championship. I felt extremely fortunate, more like a survivor than a champion.

Success in golf is finding equilibrium, accepting the fact that it is a game of ups and downs and learning something every time you tee it up. Finding that balance is a matter of trial and error. You must discover what works best for you and work diligently to maximize your potential. The difference between golf and most other sports is that anyone of average intelligence and coordination can learn to play it well. It requires a commitment to being the best that you can be. That has always been my approach to the game, for I, too, started as a blank page. Through my first teacher, my dad, the page began to fill. I absorbed as much information about the game as I possibly could. Through experimentation I started weeding out what could and could not hurt me. More important, I began to understand what worked best for me. Pop gave me many great lessons, not only about golf but also about life. His greatest advice to me was to always be myself. I pass that along to you as the first lesson in this book, which I wrote not as a panacea but as the ultimate tribute to Mom and Pop's ideal of caring and sharing. In essence, if you care for someone you'll share with them your most treasured possessions.

In this book I will share with you a lifetime, albeit a relatively short one, of knowledge about the greatest game in the world. I believe this book will assist you in attaining the deep joy and satisfaction that comes from playing the game well. I am convinced there is no game like it. In many ways it is a microcosm of life, teaching us both the

depths and heights of character. It demands integrity, promotes camaraderie, encourages good health and builds appreciation for the aesthetics. It is more than a well-struck iron or a holed putt. No, golf is not a game of perfection; it is one of reality. And keeping it real is more than a worthy goal in any endeavor.

Golf requires patience and perseverance. There are no shortcuts. Pop used to say you get out of it what you put into it. When my teacher, Butch Harmon, and I overhauled my swing during the 1998 season, Butch would sometimes have me repeat one movement for 30 minutes. I would get so tired it felt like my arms were going to fall off. But I kept at it until the move became ingrained in my muscle memory. Patience and practice

I ENJOY GIVING BACK

. . . .

My mom and dad have always been my greatest teachers and biggest supporters. They have always been there for me with sound advice that has guided me through a lot of growing pains. I learned to trust and believe in them. To me, golf instruction is similar to a parent nurturing a child. I try to get a student to emulate everything I believe is fundamentally sound. It is my obligation to share my knowledge with others because that's what I was taught.

A teacher's advice is not to be taken lightly, especially when it is proven through experience.

If my giving back to a game that has given me so much helps one person, it will be a fitting legacy to those who helped me.

pay off. So will careful attention to the techniques explained within the pages of this book—techniques I believe will work for everyone seeking to get the best out of their games. *It is structured differently from other books, beginning with the green and progressing to the tee. That's how my dad taught me, from the smallest swing to the biggest.* The instruction combines visual, kinesthetic, cognitive and performance ideals for practical application by players of all ages and abilities. Interspersed throughout the text are seven secrets I have used to elevate my game, from becoming physically stronger to mentally tougher. I believe they will work for you, too.

Ultimately, golf is a journey full of learning and discovering. I hope, through this book, you'll discover your game—one that is powerful yet precise, consistent yet exciting, impervious to pressure yet yielding large doses of fun. After all, that's the real reason we play the game. Sometimes we forget that. I did once. I was a junior golfer playing in the Orange Bowl junior tournament in Miami. I had the lead going into the final round and made a double on the front nine. I still had the lead, but for some reason I lost all joy and flat-out quit. I took my second-place trophy and pouted. Pop sternly reprimanded me. That's the only time I ever quit on golf in my life. From that time on I realized what a privilege it is to play. And I never again lost sight of why I fell for the game in the first place.

We still try because we must.

Finding a great instructor and working my butt off to improve took my game to another level.

THE
SHORT
GAME

❖ ❖ ❖

It wasn't by accident that
I learned to play golf from the
green back to the tee.

A great way to improve your feel is to putt with your eyes closed. After each putt, try to guess how far the ball rolled. This is the best drill for distance control I know of.

THE ALL-AMERICAN GRIP

I see so many types of putting grips on the pro tours these days, it gives the impression there is no "right" way to hold the putter. Maybe there isn't. The main thing in putting, whether it's with your grip, posture, stance or ball position, is to be comfortable. The putting stroke is not a very complicated action. My hands move only a foot at most in either direction during the stroke. My arms move less than that, my body less still and my head not at all. So the biggest priority in gripping the club is to establish a feeling of sensitivity, comfort and relaxation.

My putting grip is conventional in almost every way. If you look at the long history of the game and its greatest players, most of them have held the club very similarly to the way I do. I'm glad I had them as models when I was young.

IF UNIQUE IS WHAT YOU SEEK

The handle of the putter runs under the butt of my left hand. Most players like the handle running straight up the palm so the club-shaft is parallel to the left forearm. My grip is unique this way, but I believe it gives me a little extra feel and gives me freedom in my wrists when I need it.

STRAIGHT BY THE BOOK

· · · · · · · · ·

■ A bracelet I used to wear, given to me by a Buddhist monk.

■ The back of my left hand faces the target. This "weak" position discourages the hand from rotating excessively during the stroke.

■ The back of my right hand is parallel to my left hand. I don't want my hands fighting each other during the stroke. By placing both hands square to the target, it's much easier to keep the face of the putter square during the stroke, at impact especially.

■ The reverse-overlap grip, with the left forefinger laid across the fingers of the right hand, provides a sense of unity. It doesn't lock the hands together in any way, but it does prevent either hand from becoming too dominant during the stroke.

■ My right thumb extends down the shaft to a point just below my right forefinger. Any farther and my right hand and wrist tighten a bit and don't hinge freely. Any shorter and I sacrifice control.

■ I position both thumbs directly down the top of the handle. The thumbs are as sensitive as the fingers and provide the greatest amount of feedback as I swing the putter back and through the ball.

GRIP PRESSURE: EASY DOES IT

· ·

I was on the practice green with Butch Harmon one day in 1998 when Butch noticed something. "If you hold that putter any tighter, you're going to twist the grip right off it," he said with a laugh. I always listen to Butch and sure enough, I was holding the putter so firmly that I was squeezing the blood out of the tips of my fingers at address. I tried to hold the putter more lightly, but I didn't seem to have the same amount of control. And even then Butch said my grip pressure was much too intense.

A few days later, Butch showed up with a device he attached to the grip of the putter. He fooled with the setting for a minute, then challenged me to hit some putts without making the device emit a loud "beep." It went off the minute I addressed the ball. I lightened my grip pressure to quiet the thing, but when I actually went to hit a putt it went off again. Man, that thing drove me crazy. But eventually, I was able to hit putts without activating the beeper. Surprisingly, I putted pretty well with that new, light grip pressure.

Still, I wanted some reassurance that holding the club lightly was the way to go. Early in 1999, at the Byron Nelson Classic, I ran into Ben Crenshaw, who may be the greatest putter of all time. I asked him how tightly he held the putter. Ben said he gripped his putter so lightly it almost fell from his hands. "The lighter you hold it, the better you'll be able to feel the weight of the putterhead at the other end of the shaft," he said.

Hearing that from Ben did it for me. I committed myself to easing my grip pressure, and it really paid off. I shot 63-64 over the weekend and won the tournament.

HOW LIGHT IS LIGHT?

I'd say that on a scale of 1 to 10, my grip pressure is about a 5. That may be tighter than Ben holds his putter, but it's pretty light for me and I do have an increased sense of feel.

If you're having trouble on lag putts, or if your speed isn't right on shorter, breaking putts, or if you feel you're manipulating the putter, check your grip pressure. No doubt about it, light is right.

PERFECT YOUR POSTURE

. . . .

With putting, little things can make a big difference. One of the fundamentals sacred to me is posture. That applies not only to how I position my body mechanically, but also in the degree of relaxation I feel before I take the putter back.

I believe in standing fairly tall at address. That enables me to see the overall line to the hole better than when I'm stooped over close to the ground. What's more, it allows my arms to hang from my shoulder sockets in a loose, comfortable manner. That reduces tension right away. My arms also have more room to swing back and through during the stroke.

GOOD POSTURE.

DON'T HUNCH OVER.

STANCE: IT'S UP TO YOU

· · · · · · · · · · · · · · · · · ·

Because there's so little movement in your legs and torso during the stroke, the width of your stance is more a matter of comfort than anything else. Some players feel a wider stance gives them a feeling of stability and stops them from swaying. Others feel a narrow stance helps them stand more erect and gives them a better view of the line. I've varied my stance width over the years and have putted well with both a narrow stance and a wider one.

A lot of players accept the idea that they will have good days and bad days on the greens and therefore don't work at it. In fact, study and practice produce results.

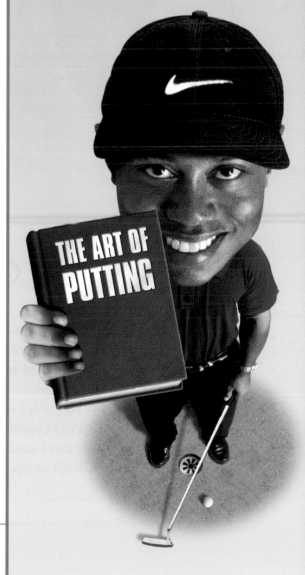

THE ART OF PUTTING

SAME ROUTINE, WITHOUT FAIL

A good putting stroke requires smooth rhythm and a steady, repeating pace. One of the secrets to accomplishing that is to do everything else smoothly and repetitively, too. I'm talking about my preputt routine, or the series of things I do before I actually pull the trigger with the putter. Regardless of your routine—and there are a lot of variations—the key is to perform it exactly the same way on every single putt.

The thing about my routine is, I never change it. I do it at the same speed and go through the same thought process every single time. Not

Here's my routine: (A) I take a general view of the putt while standing behind the ball; (B) walk to the hole, taking a side view of the line to help determine slope; (C) examine the area around the hole; (D) walk back to my ball and crouch behind it, getting the most telling view of speed and break; (E) stand alongside my ball and make two practice strokes; (F) move the putter behind the ball and then shift my feet forward; (G) take two more looks at the line and hole; and (H) stroke the putt.

only do I gather all the information I need about the putt itself, I also get myself in the best frame of mind to stroke the putt. By the time I take the putter back, I'm in a great flow, physically and mentally. That's what a good routine does for me and can do for you.

My preputt routine gets under way with a careful examination of topographical features on and around the green.

■ If there's a pond nearby, I know the ball will tend to break toward it.

■ If I'm playing a mountain course, I know the ball will tend to break away from the tallest peak in the vicinity.

Only after taking those general factors into account do I begin studying the line of the putt. To save time, I do much of my preputt routine unobtrusively while others are putting.

SAME PACE, BACK
AND THROUGH

. . . .

From the time I was a little kid—and I mean about 4 years old—my dad hammered home the idea of swinging the putter back and through at the same speed. When you see a putting stroke that looks smooth, it's because the putter is taken back at a slow, even pace and then swung forward at the same speed. If I can stroke the ball from start to finish deliberately and with a sense of rhythm, it is much easier to keep the clubhead moving along the proper path and maintain a clubface that is square to that path from start to finish. I want to avoid any sudden change in clubhead speed, especially on the forward stroke.

LET YOUR
DOMINANT HAND
RUN THE SHOW

. . . .

Although both hands are charged with swinging the putter back and through at an even pace, my dominant hand has a special responsibility. If you're right-handed, you obviously have better feel in that hand than you do in your left. Therefore, you want to instill a sense of pace with that hand especially, so it won't play too big a role in your putting stroke.

I like to hit putts with my right hand only, making sure I incorporate the same amount of pace as when I'm putting with both hands. I allow my right wrist to hinge just a bit on the backstroke and then release a little through impact. But I never allow my right wrist to "unhinge" any farther than where I had it at address. Remember, your hand leads, the clubhead trails behind.

The putter feels heavier when you hold it with one hand rather than two. Still, by holding the putter very lightly, you'll get the sense that the putter is swinging back and through almost by itself, with very little effort from your right hand.

The style of putter you use is irrelevant. The important thing is to choose a putter that hefts well in your hands and gives you a feeling of confidence just looking at it.

ALL IS WELL
AT ADDRESS.

BUT MY SWING
PATH IS TOO
FAR INSIDE—
A COMMON
PROBLEM.

THE IMPORTANCE OF SWING PATH

Once I align the face of the putter square to the target line, the most important thing is to return the clubface to that position at impact. The best way to do that is to swing the putter straight back and straight through along the same path. Speaking from personal experience, that's easier said than done. On the practice green one day, Butch told me I was swinging the putter back on an inside path. I had been putting poorly and this was the reason. Butch explained that when the putter goes back on the inside, you are forced to "release" the putterhead aggressively through impact in order to get it back to square. That causes a lot of pulls to the left and pushes to the right, not to mention inconsistent speed control.

Butch cured me fast with a little drill.

Standing to my right, down the target line, he reached forward with his own putter and placed the clubhead to the inside of the line. "Now hit the putt," he said. I did, and my putterhead collided with his on the backswing. I tried it again—same thing. It took some effort, but I finally got the putter moving straight away from the ball. I started putting better almost instantly.

The straight-back-and-through path is especially important on putts of five feet or less, where I'm not hitting the ball very hard. On longer putts, where I'm forced to turn my shoulders more in order to take the putter back farther, the putterhead tends to move to the inside a little. That's fine; I'd have to separate my arms from my body too much to keep the putter moving along the straight-back path.

FOR A LONGER PUTT, THIS IS MORE LIKE IT—SLIGHTLY INSIDE, BUT NOT MUCH.

I REGULATE DISTANCE BY VARYING THE LENGTH OF MY STROKE, NOT BY APPLYING A SUDDEN BURST OF SPEED WITH MY HANDS.

SIX KEYS TO PURE PUTTING

■ *Same Length, Back and Through*
An important key to pace and rhythm is to make my backstroke and forward stroke the same length. If I take the putter back only a few inches on a 20-footer, I'll have to accelerate suddenly to get the ball to the hole, and I'll have to lengthen my follow-through as a result.

■ *Shoulders and Arms Do Most of the Work*
The main source of movement is in the shoulders and arms. They act together; I don't want my arms running away from my shoulders at any time, in the backstroke especially. I want to keep my hands quiet during the entire stroke.

■ *Let Your Wrists Hinge—a Little*
Nothing is worse than a putting stroke that is all hands. There is too much play in the putterhead that way, and a handsy stroke doesn't hold up well under pressure. I like to keep my hands and wrists subdued during the stroke.

I don't want to freeze my hands and wrists entirely, however. If my grip pressure is light (as it should be), there is bound to be a tiny amount of hinging in my wrists. That's especially true on lag putts, where I need a longer stroke and more clubhead speed to get the ball to the hole. But keep in mind, I want to use my hands only as much as is absolutely necessary.

■ *Arms and Putter Act as One*

I want the clubshaft and my left forearm to form a straight, continuous line. To do that, I simply arch my wrists downward a little at address. By eliminating an angle between my forearms and the clubshaft, the putter will do exactly what my arms do during the stroke. The idea is to eliminate unwanted angles and levers, so the stroke is more of a one-piece action.

■ *Keep a Steady Head*

Every good putter keeps the head absolutely still from start to finish. Every bad putter I know moves the head to some degree. It's as simple as that. If I move my head even a fraction, it's almost impossible to keep my putting path stable and true. It's hard to hit the ball solidly, too. More than likely I'll open my shoulders on the forward stroke, causing me to pull the putter across the ball from out to in. I practice keeping my head dead still until well after the ball is gone.

■ *No Peeking!*

If you're like me, you can't wait to see if the ball is tracking toward the hole right after the ball leaves the putterface. But the urge to glance up too soon has some nasty consequences. The tendency to peek too soon causes my head to move and leads to sloppy contact. Not only that, if I'm distracted by thoughts of where the ball is going, I won't focus on my main job, which is to keep the putter moving directly down the target line.

I found an effective way to fight the problem: I practice putting with my left eye closed, so I can't see the target line at all with my peripheral vision. That makes it easier to keep my eyes looking straight down.

NEVER FORCE THE ISSUE

· ·

Putting is largely about touch. To really get a feel for speed, the stroke should be as easy, smooth and natural as I can make it. If I putt like a robot, stiff, locked up and too mechanical, I won't judge distance very well, especially on longer putts.

YES

Let the Toe Pass the Heel

If I keep my left arm fairly close to my side on the forward stroke, the putter-head will tend to rotate to the left after impact, the toe of the club passing the heel. I don't fight that natural tendency. The important thing is for the putterface to be square to the target line at impact, and that will happen as long as my release is smooth and unhurried.

Don't "Block It" Down the Line

Some players are so desperate to avoid pushes and pulls that they shove the putterhead down the target line, keeping the clubface dead square from start to finish. It's a very unnatural action. It doesn't do much to provide square contact, and it's almost impossible to impart the right speed consistently.

NO

than drawing your hands and arms inward toward your body through impact.

The Left-to-Right Putt: The key to this putt is to allow the putter to "release," or rotate freely, through impact. That's harder than it sounds. The tendency is to let the putterhead drift to the right (toward the hole) through impact. The result: A miss on the low side. Keep your head down, trust your line, and let the putter release naturally.

HANDLING BREAKING PUTTS

The Right-to-Left Putt: Most right-handed players prefer a putt that breaks from right to left. That's because the arms and hands are moving outward, away from the body, through impact. It's a bit more natural to stroke the ball this way, rather

LAGGING THE LONG ONES CLOSE

· · · · · · · · · · · · · · · · · ·

The only time I welcome a long putt is when I've reached a long par 5 in two. Nevertheless, I face putts of 40 feet or longer a lot more often than that, once per round on average at least. The goal, of course, is to avoid three-putting. Three-putts are killers, and that doesn't say anything about four-putting, which I've done a few times since I was a kid. (But I'm glad to say I've never five-putted!)

My goal is to lag my first putt dead to the hole, so I have nothing more than a tap-in left. That's setting the bar pretty high, but it's rare that I face a long putt so difficult that I can't lag it up there close. There are exceptions, of course. On the 17th hole at Augusta National during the Masters, they often cut the hole on the left side of the green on Sunday. That part of the green slopes severely from left to right. If I stop my approach shot on the left side of the green, forget it. I can't hit my first putt within eight feet—unless I hole it.

◄ *I make my backswing and forward stroke the same distance.*
That's the best way to assure a smooth, rhythmic stroke with plenty of feel. If my follow-through is a bit longer than my backswing, fine. But if it's shorter, I've more than likely decelerated the putter through impact, a sure killer.

◄ *I swing the putter at the same pace, back and through.*
It's important that the putter be gaining speed as it strikes the ball. But if I can feel that my putterhead is traveling at the same speed from start to finish, I'll accelerate through impact without thinking about it.

▲ *I make practice strokes while looking at the hole.*
Concentration. I see in my mind's eye the length of stroke necessary to impart the right amount of speed.

▼ **A long putt is rarely perfectly flat.**
Am I putting uphill or downhill?
As I approach the green, I look
closely to determine which
side is higher.

▲ **I study the last six feet of the putt closely.**
Knowing the way the ball behaves when
it's dying at the hole is crucial.

◄ **I hit the putt solidly at all costs.**
If I miss the sweet spot of the putterface by half an
inch—which is easy to do when I'm making an extra-
long stroke—I can lose 10 feet of roll or more.

◄ **I don't forget the break!**
I can judge the speed perfectly,
but if I push or pull the putt five
feet, I haven't done myself
any favors.

▲ **Am I putting into the grain
or downgrain?**
If I'm putting down the grain,
I can often factor in a few
extra feet of roll.

▲ **When putting up or down a tier,
I divide the putt into two sections.**
It's important that the ball arrive at the
beginning of a downhill tier with just the
right speed, and conversely, that it arrive
at the top of an uphill tier with enough
speed to get the ball to the hole.

TIGER TALE:
WHAT YOU SEE IS WHAT YOU GET

The most memorable putt of my career remains the 30-footer I buried at Pumpkin Ridge on my way to winning my third straight U.S. Amateur Championship in 1995. In the 36-hole final against Steve Scott, I stood 1 down with two holes to play. My approach shot to the 17th hole was just so-so and left me a birdie putt of about 30 feet. I read the putt carefully and was certain it would break five inches to the right. Rarely have I felt so self-assured that a putt would behave exactly as I saw it. The moment I struck the putt, I knew I had started it on line. And when it dove into the hole, I was excited but not really surprised. I'm not sure there's a strong moral to that story, except that it pays to learn how to read greens.

Reading greens is a science in that you must take into account physical factors such as the slope of the green and the type of grass you're putting on. But it's an art, too. Having competed on courses all over the world, I've experienced tremendous variations in terrain, weather, agronomy and course conditioning. They all influence how the ball rolls. Here are some rules of thumb:

■ *Fast Early, Slow Late.* Grass grows quickly—enough that the same putt you hit at 8 A.M. can be considerably slower at 5 P.M. As with all rules, however, there are exceptions. When I won the 2000 U.S. Open at Pebble Beach, the greens got quicker as the day wore on. In the morning the greens were damp and therefore slow, but when the wind came up (as it usually does), the greens dried out and got a lot faster.

■ *Learn to Read Grain.* Grass doesn't grow straight up, it tends to grow toward one side or the other. Grain isn't as big a factor as it used to be because greens are cut so short nowadays. Still, it's a factor, especially on Bermuda grass. Study the hole. One side will be shaggier than the other; a ball moving in the direction of the shaggy side will travel faster than one rolling against it. Another general rule: Grass grows toward the setting sun.

■ *Wind Can Matter.* When it's blowing more than 15 m.p.h., pay attention. A golf ball weighs only a little more than an ounce and a half, so you can bet it can be influenced by the wind.

■ *Balls Roll Where Water Drains.* If there's a pond near the green, I can be sure the ball will favor moving in that direction.

■ *Mountains Are Mystifying.* If I'm playing a mountain course, strange things can happen. Putts that appear straight will break for no apparent reason. The rule: Find the highest mountain peak in the vicinity; the green will tend to slope away from it.

NARROW YOUR WORLD

A few years ago, I started cupping my hands around my eyes while I read putts. The reason I do it is not because I see more, it's because I see less. The PGA Tour can get some pretty big galleries, and there's always a lot of movement I sometimes find distracting. By forming a little tunnel with my hands, I can focus totally on reading my line.

You probably don't have too big a crowd watching you play, but still there are distractions—carts zooming around, fellows walking around the greens and so forth. If you have trouble concentrating, try my "tunnel vision" technique. It will sharpen your focus and help you hole more putts.

❖2❖
HOW TO GET IT DOWN

TURNING THREE INTO TWO

I don't think I've ever felt more pressure than the day our Western High School golf team was going up against our big crosstown rival to decide our district championship. We were playing at Los Coyotes Country Club in Buena Park, Calif., a nice course that has played host to the LPGA Tour. Our matches were only nine holes and were played at stroke play, with everybody's score counting. I was playing well and came to the last hole four under par. But the match was very close. When I saw my coach and teammates gathered around the par-3 ninth green, I knew what I did on that hole could very possibly spell the difference between our team winning or losing.

My tee shot sailed over the green, leaving me a tricky little downhill pitch from light rough. My ball was sitting up nicely. I figured I would have no trouble hitting a little flop shot up close to the hole, from where I would make the putt for par and lead my team to glory.

I addressed the ball with my sand wedge, opening my stance and the clubface. Taking a deep breath, I made a healthy-sized backswing, cut across the ball firmly—and whiffed the shot. My lie, as it turned out, had been too good. The clubhead had slid right under the ball.

Now I faced an even more difficult shot, because the ball had settled lower into the rough. Feeling more angry than scared, I settled over the ball again and played the same type of shot, a high-risk flop. This time I holed it out! I saved a par and our team pulled out the title.

Two lessons were driven home to me that afternoon, lessons my dad had pounded into my head for years. The first is, a good short game can save a round regardless of how poorly you're hitting the ball from tee to green. The second lesson had to do with that whiff. That terrible shot, where I failed to judge the quality of the lie correctly, made it clear that I could never reach my full potential unless I built a reliable short game.

As you'll see, there's more to getting up and down than you may think.

THE STATS TELL THE STORY

The thing I'll remember about my 2000 season was that I performed well in all facets of my game. Not having any really weak areas was the reason I won eight tournaments, was the leading

I missed hitting in regulation, I made par or better on two of them from all kinds of tough situations around the greens. If I had stumbled in that category, it would have cost me a few tournaments, the Vardon Trophy and a whole bunch of money.

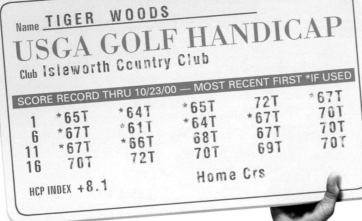

money-winner, took home three major championships, won the Vardon Trophy for low stroke average, and was named Player of the Year. But it was my short game that made the biggest contribution.

I ranked first in the Greens In Regulation category, hitting better than three greens out of every four with my approaches. That adds up to just under 14 greens per round, my best percentage ever.

I also ranked first in putting. That's a telling stat, because if you're hitting lots of greens and making lots of putts, you're making lots of birdies.

The Scrambling category, where I ranked third over all, was the real key and proves how important the short game is to scoring. When I missed the green, I got up and down for par or better 67.1 percent of the time. So, of the four greens per round

THE BASIC CHIP: NOTHING FANCY

O nce you establish a good chipping technique, the battle is 90 percent over. Whether you're chipping uphill or downhill, whether the shot is long or short or whether the lie is perfect or a little scruffy, to be a good chipper you need sound fundamentals. Some shots around the green are trickier than others, but they all revolve around the same simple approach.

■ I set my hands slightly ahead of the ball.

■ I grip the club as I do the putter. I don't need a lot of hand action.

■ I lean a little toward the target. That promotes a downward blow, too.

■ I choke down on the club for extra control.

■ I flex my knees a little. I want my legs to feel alive.

■ I narrow my stance. I don't need a wide base of support.

■ I position the ball slightly back of center. That promotes a downward blow into the back of the ball.

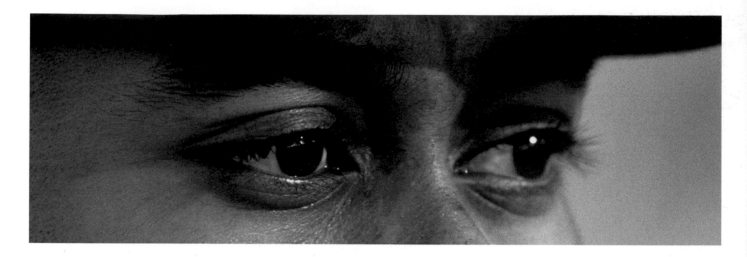

SEE THE SHOT HAPPEN BEFORE YOU HIT IT

. . . .

The chip, like a putt, requires an advance "read." But I'm looking for more than how the ball will behave after it lands on the green. To control distance accurately (that's much harder to do than start the ball on line), I choose a spot where I want the ball to land, and then form a mental picture of the ball actually traveling there.

Ready to Go

■ I hold the club softly and make sure there's no tension in my arms.

■ I open my stance to the target line. I see the line better, and it helps limit action to my arms and shoulders.

■ I keep my chin held high, my back straight. A lot of bad chippers hunch down over the ball.

■ I hold the club very lightly at address.

GIVE IT THE OLD 1-2

. . . .

The chipping stroke is simple. It's an easy one-two action controlled by the shoulders more than the arms and hands. You don't need much force. My goal is to hit the ball solidly, making sure the clubhead is traveling downward at the moment it strikes the ball.

■ I start the backswing with my shoulders, allowing my arms and hands to follow. I don't let my arms separate too far from my body. Tempo is important; there's no need to rush on either the backswing or forward swing.

■ At all costs, I hit down on the back of the ball. I don't try to help the ball into the air—the loft of the club will take care of that for me.

■ The stroke may be short, but it's not a stab. I try to accelerate smoothly.

■ A good thought is to return the arms to the position they were in at address. That means, my hands are ahead of the ball. No scooping!

■ I keep my eyes focused on the back of the ball. After impact, my eyes stay focused on that same point.

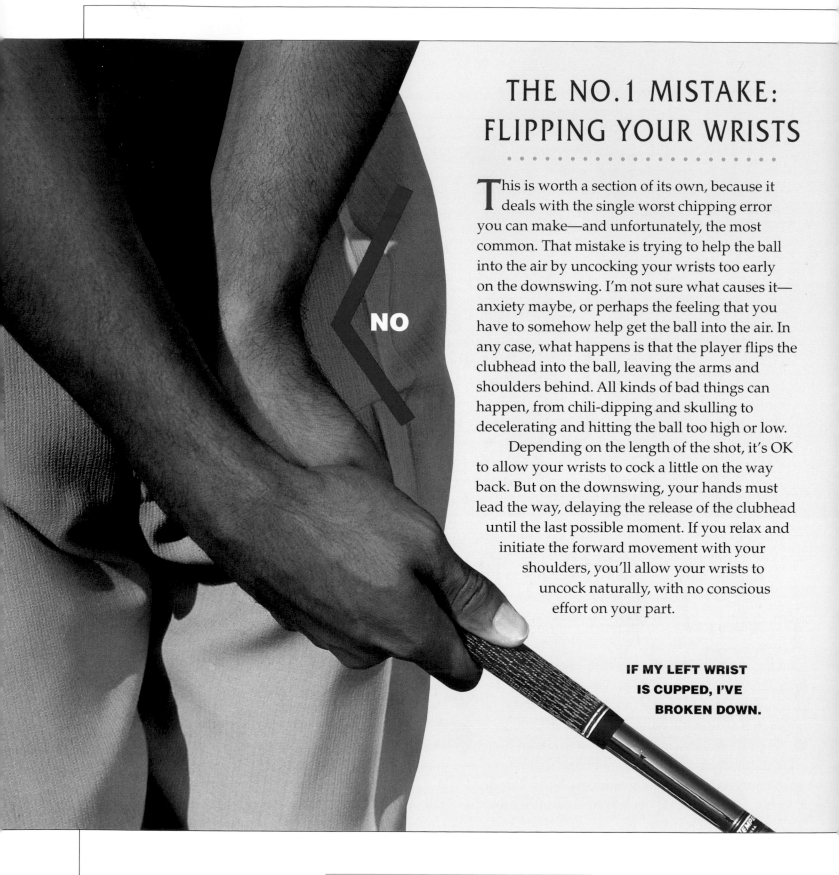

THE NO.1 MISTAKE: FLIPPING YOUR WRISTS

· ·

NO

This is worth a section of its own, because it deals with the single worst chipping error you can make—and unfortunately, the most common. That mistake is trying to help the ball into the air by uncocking your wrists too early on the downswing. I'm not sure what causes it—anxiety maybe, or perhaps the feeling that you have to somehow help get the ball into the air. In any case, what happens is that the player flips the clubhead into the ball, leaving the arms and shoulders behind. All kinds of bad things can happen, from chili-dipping and skulling to decelerating and hitting the ball too high or low.

Depending on the length of the shot, it's OK to allow your wrists to cock a little on the way back. But on the downswing, your hands must lead the way, delaying the release of the clubhead until the last possible moment. If you relax and initiate the forward movement with your shoulders, you'll allow your wrists to uncock naturally, with no conscious effort on your part.

**IF MY LEFT WRIST
IS CUPPED, I'VE
BROKEN DOWN.**

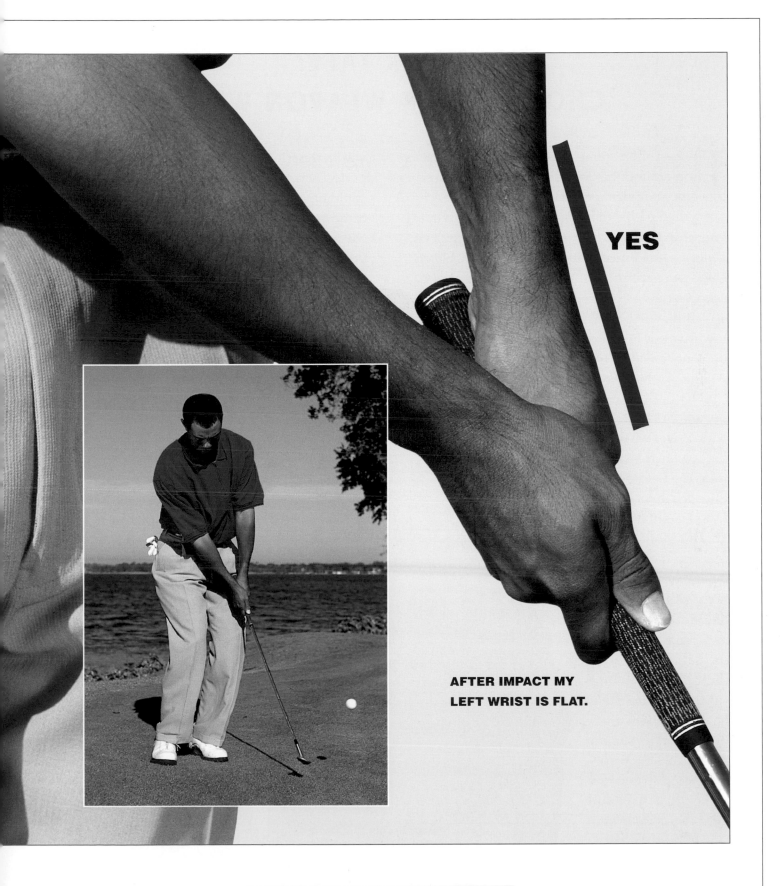

YES

AFTER IMPACT MY
LEFT WRIST IS FLAT.

TIGER TALE:
CHOOSE YOUR WEAPON WISELY

The best short-game artists vary their club selection around the greens. They vary the speed, trajectory and distance of ball flight with the club, not with the type of stroke they make. If it's a long chip that requires more roll than flight, I will choose a less-lofted club, such as a 7-iron. Shorter chips can require anything up to a 60-degree sand wedge.

Still, you probably are going to lean toward your favorite chipping club. My personal choice is my 56-degree sand wedge. At the 1998 Million Dollar Challenge in South Africa, I found myself locked in an intense duel against Nick Price. We both had gone low that day and had separated ourselves from the field. At one point on the back nine, Nick birdied five straight holes and I birdied four of the same five and then birdied the next. We came to the last hole with me trailing by one stroke.

Nick hit the green on that last hole and I didn't, although I was closer to the hole than he was. Nick two-putted for his par and now it was my turn— hole the chip and enter a playoff, or miss and take the long plane ride home. My ball was in the fringe 30 feet from the hole, sitting perfectly with a beautiful run to the hole. I really could have used any club for that shot—an 8-iron came to mind, then a pitching wedge, then my trusty sand wedge. All things being equal, I preferred my sand wedge. I just like the look and feel of it. I chose a spot on the green to land the ball, went through my routine, got set and hit the ball perfectly. It landed on the spot I had chosen, hopped once, started rolling and took the little right-to-left break perfectly. It dove into the middle of the hole and we played off for the title—which incidentally, was worth more than a million dollars.

Nick, unfazed by my chip, won that playoff. But my point is, don't be afraid to have a small bias toward your favorite chipping club. As long as your favorite club can deliver the correct type of shot, you're allowed to deviate from the norm.

HOW TO HANDLE GREENSIDE ROUGH

. . . .

Tall grass around the greens intimidates most golfers, and understandably so. For me it's one of the hardest shots there is, though I've gotten much better at it. At the 2000 U.S. Open at Pebble Beach, I landed in the tall stuff a few times, but managed to save par almost every time.

■ I use my 60-degree wedge. The tall grass tends to close the clubface, and I need all the loft I can get.

■ I distribute 60 percent of my weight on my forward foot—the one closest to the green. That encourages a steep, knifelike angle of attack with the clubhead.

■ I hold the club more firmly than normal, especially with my left hand. Again, the rough will try to twist the clubface closed.

■ I make a very upright backswing, cocking my wrists abruptly.

■ On the downswing, the force of the clubhead should be expended *downward*, to penetrate the grass. I don't let the clubhead approach the ball on a level angle; I'd be at the mercy of the rough.

■ I restrict my follow-through. In fact, if I hit down sharply, there won't *be* any follow-through.

THE 3-WOOD CHIP: A FOOLPROOF TECHNIQUE

Butch Harmon taught me this shot early in the week of the 1996 U.S. Open at Oakland Hills, and I can't think of one that had a bigger immediate impact on my game. The first time I tried it, on the 18th hole of the third round, I actually holed the shot. At Quad Cities later that year, I holed out using the 3-wood chip three times. It's a much easier shot to play than most players would think.

When to Play the Shot

The 3-wood chip is a good choice when your ball is in the fringe or in short, light rough around the green. It's effective because the broad sole of the 3-wood will resist getting snagged by the rough near impact. What's more, the 3-wood has enough loft to carry the ball a few feet onto the green, from where it rolls like a putt the rest of the way to the hole. Don't try this shot if your ball is sitting down in deep rough. Size up the situation carefully before you grab that lofted wood from your bag.

"Pop" the Clubface Into the Ball

I keep my left hand relaxed. I take the clubhead away from the ball low, so it brushes the top of the grass. I use my wrists to pop the clubface into the back of the ball, keeping the back of my left hand moving down the target line. I don't feel like I'm jabbing at the ball with the clubhead. I just accelerate the clubhead more quickly than usual. The worst thing you can do is let the clubhead slow down just before impact.

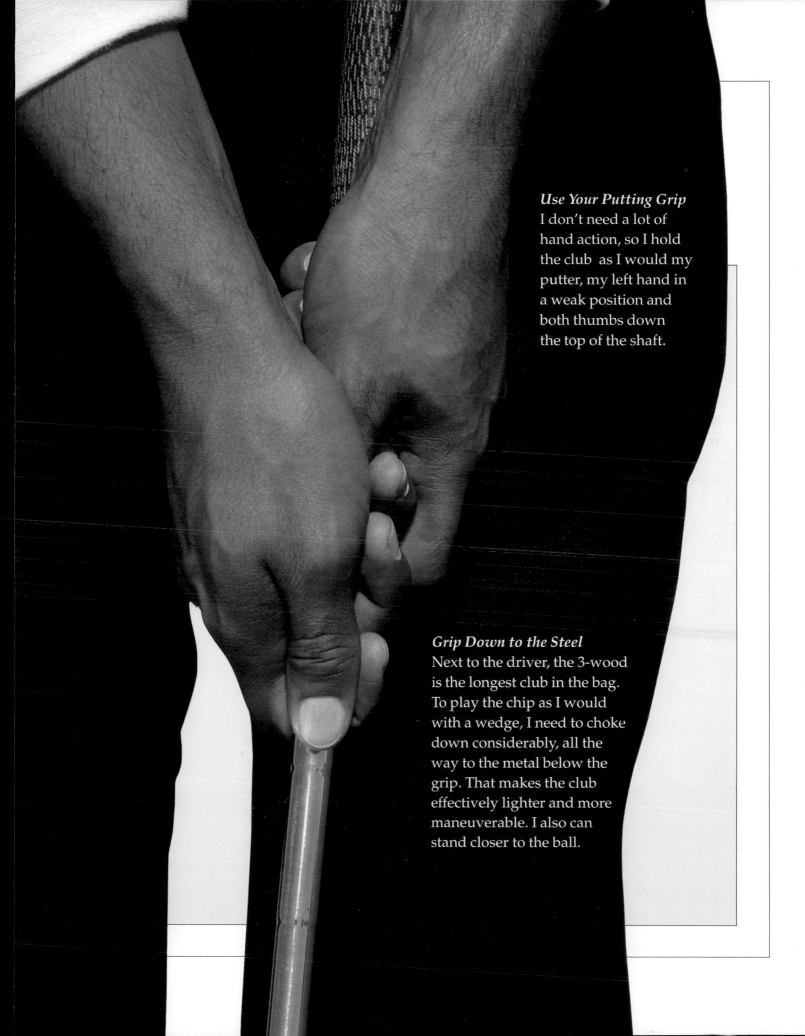

Use Your Putting Grip
I don't need a lot of
hand action, so I hold
the club as I would my
putter, my left hand in
a weak position and
both thumbs down
the top of the shaft.

Grip Down to the Steel
Next to the driver, the 3-wood
is the longest club in the bag.
To play the chip as I would
with a wedge, I need to choke
down considerably, all the
way to the metal below the
grip. That makes the club
effectively lighter and more
maneuverable. I also can
stand closer to the ball.

THE SIMPLE PITCH

. . . .

The pitch is not a long shot, but it requires a lot more hand, arm and body action than the chip shot. That's because you need more clubhead speed to get the ball in the air. It really is like a mini version of the full swing. Even your lower body plays a role, as the hips turn slightly back and through to accommodate the motion in your shoulders, arms and hands. It's a delicate balance; you need enough momentum to slide the club-head through the grass and under the ball, but not so much as to rocket the ball over the green.

Preprogram the Desired Loft
The secret to hitting the ball high and soft is not to force it. Four preswing adjustments will help you a lot:

1. Choose a lofted club, either your standard sand wedge or 60-degree wedge.

2. Open your stance by aligning your feet well left of the target line.

3. Open the clubface to increase loft.

4. Play the ball forward, off your left toe.

Keep Everything Moving

My main downswing thought is to slide the club-head under the ball. I make sure I accelerate—if I allow the clubhead to stop, I'll probably chunk the shot. I don't rotate my hands and the clubhead dramatically through impact. On the follow-through, the clubface should be aiming at the sky, proof I've maintained the loft of the clubface.

Focus on Your Hands

The hands are much more active on the pitch than on the chip. I strengthen my left-hand grip a bit by turning it to my left at address—that will enable my hands to cock more easily during the swing. It's crucial that I hold the club lightly, both for mobility and feel.

Let the Club Do the Work

The rest is easy. I pick the club up steeply on the backswing, allowing my wrists to cock naturally. Watch my tempo—I'm not making a long swing, but it still needs to be smooth and rhythmic.

THE 30-YARD PUNCH

. . . .

One of the hardest shots to master (and one every golfer faces virtually every round) is the short punch from about 30 yards from the green. Like any shot that requires something less than a full swing, you need good technique and a soft touch to pull it off.

I position my ball just back of center, which helps me hit down on the ball. I narrow my stance so my feet are between the width of my shoulders; I don't need a wide, stable base because I won't be making a very long swing.

I start the swing low and wide, making sure my left arm is fully extended. I always remember to turn my shoulders and hips a little, too.

BACKSWING IS LOW AND WIDE.

ARMS ARE STILL IN FRONT OF MY BODY.

Big Muscles Guide a Short Swing

I never try to swing through the ball with my arms and hands alone, because it's too difficult to control the loft of the clubface and regulate clubhead speed. My thought is to simply unturn my hips and let them guide my shoulders, arms and hands through the downswing. A low, abbreviated finish is my goal—it proves the big muscles have directed the motion, not my arms and hands.

With this basic technique, I can play any variety of short shots. By moving my ball position forward a touch and choosing one of my sand wedges, I can loft the ball high. By playing the ball even farther back and choosing a less-lofted club, I can play the bump-and-run.

THE FLOP: MAKING THE HARD LOOK EASY

. . . .

No doubt about it, the flop shot is a high-risk gamble. I only play it when I have very little green to work with or when it's the only way to get the ball close to the hole. Still, it's a shot every golfer needs to have. The nature of modern design features around many greens demands it.

I Open My Stance, Play the Ball Forward

My stance and clubface are both open at address, with the ball played off my left heel. I grip the club more lightly than normal, to promote lots of hand speed on the downswing. I like a wide stance because it forces me to execute the shot from the waist up. The swing is 90 percent shoulders, arms and hands.

Short Shot, Long Swing

On the backswing, I pick the club up steeply and cup my left wrist into a slightly concave "V"—that opens the clubface even farther, which guarantees maximum loft through impact. I make a long swing, again to help generate speed. I accelerate quickly through impact, trying to slide the club under the ball. I remember to follow through; I don't want to chop at the ball.

When I'm chipping uphill, I usually prefer to take the flagstick out of the hole. Downhill, it's just the opposite—I leave it in so it can behave like a backstop if I chip a little strong.

THWAK!

❖3❖
HOW TO ESCAPE FROM SAND

MAKING THE HARD EASY

There are tough shots, and then there was the one I had on the 16th hole at Poipu Bay Resort in Hawaii during the 1997 Grand Slam of Golf. With three holes to play, I was trailing Ernie Els by three shots and desperately needed a birdie to have even an outside chance of catching him. When I saw my approach to 16 drop into the right greenside bunker, I knew a birdie would be unlikely, but not impossible. I'd holed sand shots before.

But when I got close enough to observe my lie, I saw a shot that was close to impossible. The ball had buried into the thick, wet sand. Worse, it was on a severe downslope. To get the ball out of the bunker would be very difficult, and if I did there was no way it was going to hold the green. A thick clump of bushes beyond the green was beckoning to my ball. I was a dead man.

Or was I? A steep, grassy embankment was just beyond the bunker. If I could somehow make the ball fly directly into the embankment, the ball might release forward and get on the green. It was a 100-1 shot, but I had to try it.

I addressed the ball as though I were ready to chop wood. I didn't swing the club back so much as lift it straight in the air, then brought it down into the sand as though I were swinging an ax. I swung as hard as I could, closing my eyes tight, and hoped for the best.

When I found the courage to peek at the outcome, I saw an amazing sight. The ball had shot straight forward like a bullet and slammed into the embankment. The ball jumped into the air a good three feet and continued forward, stopping two feet from the hole. I knocked the putt in for one of the best pars of my life, and very proudly tipped my cap to the gallery. Even Ernie congratulated me. Ernie parred the hole and held on to win by three. But that sand shot, which ranks as one of the best I've ever played in my life, made my day and eased the pain of losing.

THE NO-FAIL SETUP

More than for any other shot in golf, the setup for the standard bunker shot determines the type of swing I make and the way the club behaves when it enters the sand. It's a four-part process.

I Open My Stance
I align everything—my feet, hips and shoulders—to the left of the target. That preprograms an out-to-in swing, the clubhead cutting across the sand and the ball through impact.

I Open the Clubface
I aim the clubface to the right of the target the amount you see here. That does two things: It increases the loft of the clubface so I can hit the ball high and soft, and it also increases the amount of "bounce" on the sole of the clubhead.

I Weaken My Grip
The last thing I want on a sand shot is for the clubface to rotate to a closed position through impact. To discourage that rotation, I weaken my left-hand grip at address, so the back of my left hand faces the target.

I Position the Ball Forward
I like it just opposite my left heel. Playing the ball forward promotes a higher trajectory, and also encourages me to slide the clubhead easily through the sand.

EASY DOES IT

Remember one thing: The standard bunker shot is about technique, not about strength. I don't apply any more effort than I would on a 40-yard shot from the fairway.

I Downsize My Swing

I don't need a long swing with lots of body action, as there is no need for extra distance. I keep my grip pressure light, maintain an easy rhythm and swing my hands back to about shoulder height.

I Cock My Wrists Fully

The clubhead speed I generate comes mainly from my hands and arms. I break my wrists early on the backswing and cock them all the way. This is a very "handsy" shot, with very little movement in my hips and legs.

I'm a Right-Hand Man

The swing on the greenside bunker shot is dominated by the right hand. Through impact, the action is very similar to throwing a ball.

I Go Ahead and Release

Even though I've really slung the club through the sand with my right hand, you'll notice that the toe of the clubhead hasn't turned over fully after impact. That's due to my weak left-hand grip. I know the ball will come out high and soft.

I Slide, I Don't Chop

See how the sand is being thrown forward on a fairly low angle? That's because I haven't hit down too steeply on the ball. I simply try to swing through impact into the follow-through, the ball coming out on a small cushion of sand.

HOW MUCH SAND DO I TAKE?

· ·

The amount of sand I take depends on how much spin I want to put on the ball. I've drawn lines to indicate where the clubhead should enter the sand, which determines how much backspin I will apply. When I want the ball to run after it hits the green, I aim for a spot about three inches behind the ball. The ball then comes out on a thick cushion of sand with hardly any backspin.

When I want to hit the ball high and make it stop quickly, I'll hit maybe an inch behind the ball, sometimes less. I very rarely try to pick the ball cleanly without taking any sand at all, as the ball can very easily get away from me and fly too far.

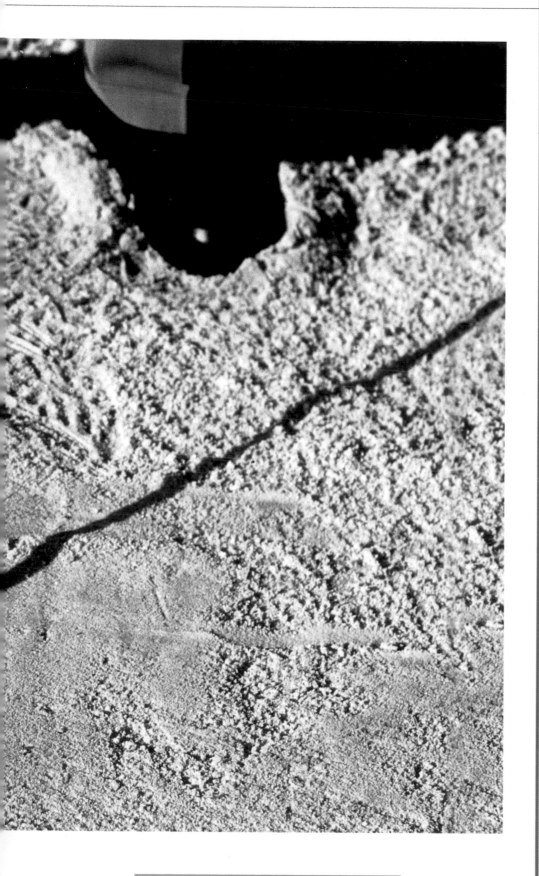

The rules permit you to remove a man-made object (such as a cigarette butt) from the bunker, but you can't remove natural objects such as a twig or leaf.

SCRATCH SCRATCH

WHY THE SAND WEDGE WORKS

. . . .

The sand wedge has the most distinctive design of any club in the bag. It is very well-suited for sand, because the design prevents the clubhead from digging too deeply, which would cause me to flub the shot. Note the side-by-side comparison between a typical sand wedge and its closest relative, the pitching wedge.

■ The flange along the sole of the clubhead extends lower than the leading edge. That causes the club to behave like a rudder when it strikes the sand, skidding through it easily instead of penetrating too deeply.

■ The flange also is wider from back to front than the soles of the other irons. That's another reason it glides through the sand rather than digging deeply into it.

■ The sand wedge is the shortest club in the bag (except for your putter), and is also the heaviest. That extra mass helps the clubhead penetrate the sand just far enough to slide under the ball.

■ The sand wedge has more loft than any other club, anywhere from 52 degrees to more than 60. When I'm playing from a greenside bunker to a pin cut near the edge of the green, I need as much height on the shot as possible.

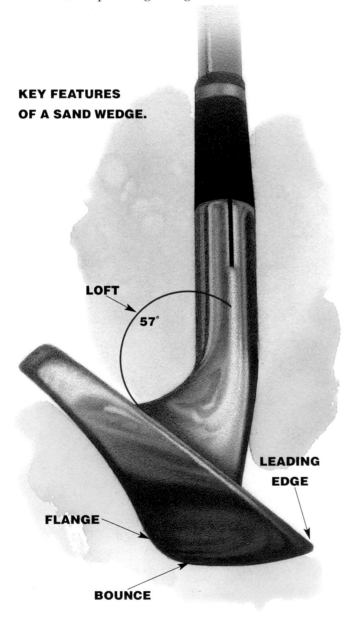

KEY FEATURES OF A SAND WEDGE.

LOFT

57°

LEADING EDGE

FLANGE

BOUNCE

I ALWAYS ACCELERATE

. . . .

If there is one mistake common among poor bunker players, it's decelerating through impact. It probably stems from hitting at the ball instead of through it. To be consistent from sand, the clubhead must be gaining speed when it enters the sand instead of slowing down. This is true even on short bunker shots. I try to imagine that the club is traveling its fastest at a point six inches beyond the ball.

I GO AFTER
IT HARD WITH
MY RIGHT HAND.

A PRIMER ON THE BURIED LIE

A ball buried in sand can work on your mind. Remember that shot I pulled off from a buried lie at the Grand Slam of Golf in Hawaii? When I first saw that the ball was buried, I didn't exactly look forward to playing it. I won't lie; I was discouraged. Not only did I have an awkward stance, but the fact that the ball was buried meant I would have limited control over how the ball behaved when I hit it. I realized I would need a lot of luck just to get up and down and that a birdie was almost out of the question. It was all I could do to pull myself together and apply everything I had into playing that shot.

At first blush, buried lies bum all of us out.

Truth is, buried lies aren't all that difficult to play—if you don't count that lucky shot I pulled off in Hawaii. Sure, you won't hit the ball as close to the hole consistently as you would from a perfect lie, but you can still hit the ball close enough to have a reasonable chance at an up-and-down.

I Hit the Spot
To get the ball out of a plugged lie, I have to find a way to make the club penetrate

1.
THIS IS WHERE THE CLUB ENTERS THE SAND.

2.
I LINE UP TO THE LEFT...

3.
AND PUNCH DOWN FIRMLY.

the sand as deeply as possible. I want to take a divot that is deep enough to bury a small animal in. I like to aim for a spot about two inches behind the ball—that's where the divot starts.

I Open Up and Lean to the Left
I'm going to need a very vertical swing, the club entering the sand on as steep an angle as possible. I adjust my setup accordingly: (1) I address the ball with an open stance to encourage a steep, out-to-in swing path; (2) I lean to my left so my spine is more vertical as opposed to being slanted

to my right; (3) I open the clubface and position my hands ahead of the ball.

Forget Finesse!
This is no time to make a soft, cozy swing. I put a lot of effort into the shot, applying extra force with my right hand. Remember, I swing down as opposed to through the shot. I'll have almost no follow-through because the sand will stop the clubhead less than a foot after impact. The ball will come out with almost no spin, so I allow for extra run.

THE HARDEST SHOT IN GOLF

· ·

No doubt about it, the toughest shot to play well consistently is the long explosion. By long, I mean a shot of about 30 yards—too long to play with your green-side bunker technique, too short to play like you would a full shot from a fairway bunker. There is an effective way to play it, but even after I show you how, you're going to need lots of practice. I experiment with different clubs, too. For a 30-yard shot I'll use anything from a sand wedge to an 8-iron depending on the lie.

I Modify My Setup
Because this shot requires as much body action as a full-swing shot from the fairway, I set up with my feet and shoulders open very slightly to the target line. I don't want to be so open that I can't turn freely, but I am open enough to make the clubhead approach the ball on a head-on path instead of from inside the target line.

Clubface Is Square, Ball Slightly Forward
Opening the clubface increases loft, and I don't want to hit the ball so high that it can't travel far enough forward to reach the green. So I set the clubface square to the target line. I also will want to take just a little sand on this shot, so I aim about an inch behind the ball (note line in sand). Precision is everything. Take more sand than that, and I'll come up short. Hit the ball thin, I'll airmail the green.

I Swing with Controlled Fury
I'll need as much clubhead speed as I can muster, so I'll want to make as big a back-swing as I comfortably can. But remember what I said about precision—I make sure I keep my head still, and maintain a smooth tempo. I swing through the ball with lots of acceleration, arriving at a full, complete finish.

DIALING IN
MY DISTANCE

· ·

Making the transition from a short sand shot to a longer one is pretty tricky. A lot of players regulate their distance by opening or closing the clubface, or else varying how much sand they take. I prefer to regulate how far the ball flies by adjusting the length of my follow-through. The longer the shot, the harder I try to achieve a full, complete finish. This little trick is very effective, because in order to lengthen my follow-through, I have to accelerate pretty fiercely through impact. On the other hand, a short follow-through means I haven't swung all out through impact and the ball won't travel as far.

FOR QUICK HEIGHT, MAINTAIN LOFT

· · · · · · · · · · · · · · · ·

One of the things I love about playing in the British Open is the unique course design features you see in Scotland and England. The most dramatic may be the steep, sod-faced bunkers that are easy to get into and brutal trying to escape from. I try to avoid these monstrosities at almost any cost, because you sometimes are forced to play sideways to get out of one, and I don't like throwing away strokes. I'm getting good at avoiding them, too—when I won the 2000 British Open at St. Andrews, I didn't land in one all week.

That wasn't the case at Carnoustie, where the British Open was played in 1999 and where the above photo was taken. The picture shows how I pulled the shot off. See how the face of my sand wedge is still facing skyward? That shows I maintained the loft of the clubface, never allowing the clubhead to turn over through impact. And look at how much sand I took. That shows the importance of penetrating the sand deeply enough for the clubhead to slide under the ball and get it up in the air.

If your lie is suspect, it's better to play the ball farther back in your stance than farther forward.

SOME
EXPLOSIVE
THOUGHTS

. . . .

I believe the principles of good sand play are pretty much the same for everyone. If you want to hit the ball higher, there's no arguing that you must either open the club-face or position the ball farther forward in your stance to increase your launch angle. I mean, there's no other sound way to obtain more height on the shot.

There are other principles that have more to do with strategy and club selection than with physics and swing mechanics. Every amateur (high handicappers especially) should obey the following rules at all times.

■ From fairway bunkers, forget about using any club longer than a 4-iron unless the sand is moist and packed, with the ball perched in a perfect lie.

■ Another fairway bunker tip: Take at least one club more than you would from grass at the same distance.

■ The longer the shot, the lighter you should hold the club. That increases your ability to generate speed, and speed is necessary on every shot from sand.

■ If your lie is even a little dicey, position the ball at least an inch farther back in your stance than you would from a perfect lie. If the lie is bad, play it back even farther.

■ From greenside bunkers, aim for the top of the flagstick—most misses from sand come up short rather than long, so give yourself the benefit of the doubt.

THE FULL SWING

❖ ❖ ❖

*My swing is a work in
progress and always will be,
starting with sound basics.*

❖4❖
HOW TO SWING

BUILDING AN ACTION TO LAST

After I won the 1997 Masters by 12 strokes with a record score of 270, 18 under par, I wasted no time before celebrating. I do know how to have fun, and I didn't leave anything in the bag. I partied with my buddies, traveled a little and generally had a great time. I knew I would have to come back to earth eventually, but I wasn't in any special hurry to get there.

One night, a week or so later, after the elation had started to die down, I decided to sit down and watch a tape of the entire tournament. I was by myself, so I was really able to concentrate on critiquing my full swing to see if there was some flaw I might be able to work on.

I didn't see one flaw. I saw about 10.

I had struck the ball great that week, but by my standard I felt I had gotten away with murder. My clubshaft was across the line at the top of the backswing and my clubface was closed. My swing plane was too upright. I liked my ball flight, but I was hitting the ball farther with my irons than I should have been because I was delofting the clubface through impact. I didn't like the look of those things, and the more I thought about it, the more I realized I didn't like how my swing felt, either. From a ball-striking standpoint, I was playing better than I knew how.

Even before the tape ended, I committed myself to making some big changes in my swing. Butch had pointed out some of these swing flaws before, and we had been working on them slowly, but I decided right then and there to pick up the pace. I got on the phone and called Butch and let him know what I was thinking. He was all for the swing overhaul I had in mind.

That overhaul took more than a year before the changes really started to kick in. First, my full swing started to look better. Then, the ball started to behave better. Finally, my swing started to feel right, and that's when I knew I had it. I had a very good year in 1999, and in 2000 I played by far the best golf of my life.

The point to this story is, the golf swing will always be a work in progress regardless of how good you are. The goal is to have a swing that is mechanically sound, repeatable, works with every club in your set and holds up under pressure. I don't know if anyone will ever achieve a state of perfection—I know I haven't. But you can bet I'll keep trying.

ONE GRIP FOR ALL SHOTS

. . . .

The grip is the cornerstone of the swing. It is related to almost every element of the swing itself, including path, clubface position, ball position and posture. It isn't really necessary to explain how the grip relates to these other factors, except to say that to have a chance of building a good swing, you need a good grip.

My own grip has evolved over the years. When I was a junior golfer, I preferred a strong left-hand grip, my hand rotated well to my right on the handle of the club. That made both hands much more active during the swing, made it easier to square the clubface at impact, and gave me extra distance. Later, after I grew and became stronger, I weakened my left hand considerably. Today it's in a fairly neutral position, with 2 1/2 knuckles of my left hand showing at address. That's the best position of all in my opinion, and one I know will suit most every golfer.

Whenever I made a grip change, I made sure I had a club in my hands constantly so I could "practice" my new grip. I wanted my new grip to start feeling natural as quickly as possible.

In choosing a particular player to model your swing after, take into consideration the player's height and build. If you're tall and thin, you don't want to copy the swing of a player who is short and stocky.

MY LEFT HAND IS MY CONTROL HAND

• •

The handle of the club runs diagonally across the base of my fingers, from the base of the fore-finger to a point atop the callus pad below my little finger. That provides the best combination of sensitiv-ity and control. At all costs, I avoid placing the handle too far toward the palm of my open left hand. I'll lose clubhead speed and the sensitivity I refer to.

When the left-hand grip is complete and I lower the club into the address position, my thumb should be positioned to the right of center on the handle, and the "V" formed by my right thumb and forefinger should point just outside my right ear.

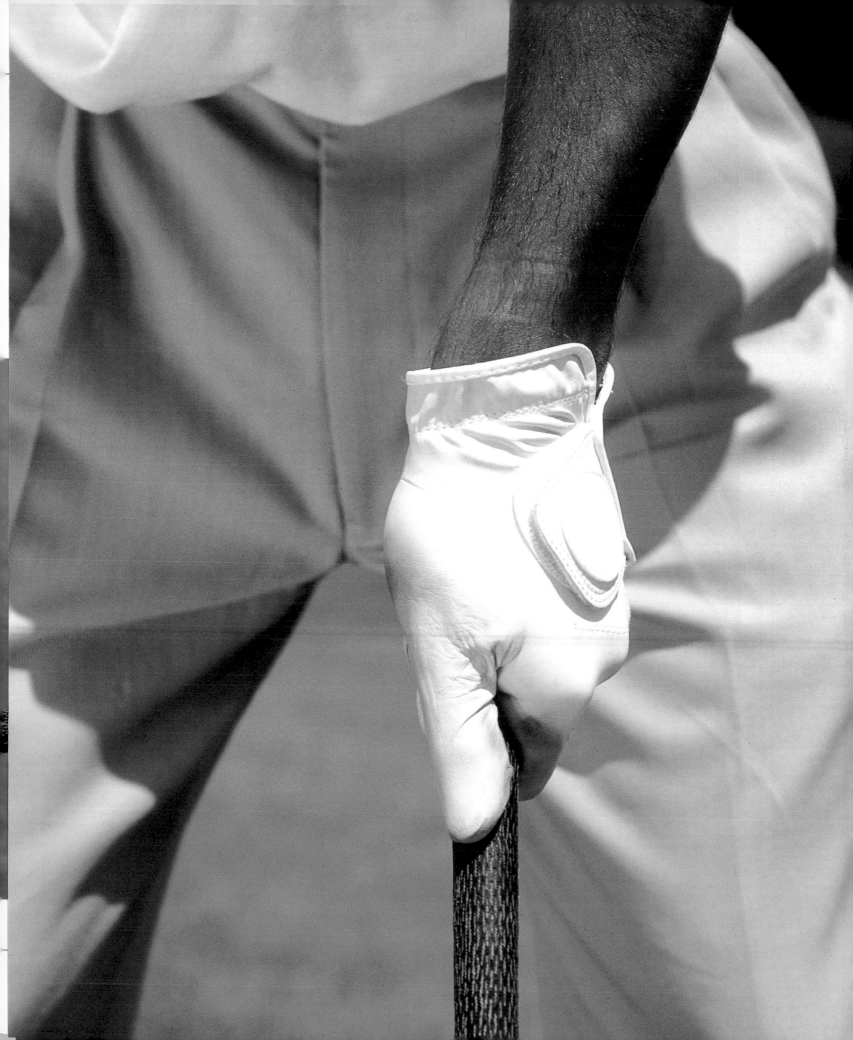

Never judge your practice sessions on how long you practiced or how many balls you hit. Some of my most productive practice sessions have lasted all of 20 minutes.

THE FINISHED PRODUCT

My complete grip provides a sense of snugness and unity between the two hands. They should feel as if they are melded together, almost as if you were born to hold a club. If you don't have that sensation, practice gripping and regripping the club. Keep a club handy just for this purpose.

You should hold the club lightly enough to allow plenty of wrist freedom and to have some feel, but firmly enough to maintain control of the club throughout the swing. The most important thing is to keep your grip pressure steady. If you increase your grip pressure at any point during the swing, it will cost you clubhead speed and control of the club.

On the subject of grip pressure, I believe a lot of amateurs hold the club too tightly because their hands aren't on the club correctly to begin with. To prevent the club from sliding around the fingers and palm, they instinctively tighten their hold, usually at the beginning of the downswing. It proves once again why a technically perfect grip is so important. If your grip is sound, you don't have to think about your hands at all during the swing. You're free to concentrate on the other aspects of good ball striking.

STANCE IS FOR BALANCE—AND POWER

The full swing involves a lot of motion in your upper body. You need a solid foundation to support that motion without stifling it, and that's where stance width comes in.

My Feet Are Too Narrow

This stance width, with my feet about shoulder-width apart, is fine for the short and middle irons. For the driver and fairway woods, however, it's too narrow. There's no way I could maintain my balance and stability with my feet this close together. To do it, I would have to swing at half speed.

My Feet Are Too Wide

Here I have plenty of stability—you'd have a hard time knocking me over if you tried. But remember, the wider your stance, the more you restrict the turning of your hips and shoulders on the back and forward swings.

The Proper Stance Width

Here's a nice blend. For this driver shot, the insides of my feet line up with the outside points of my shoulders. From here I can swing all out with plenty of support from my feet and legs, while at the same time maintaining my ability to turn my hips and shoulders fully.

The right stance width allows me to shift my weight onto my right side while maintaining the flex in my right knee. I'm balanced, fully loaded and ready to go after it on the downswing.

DISTANCE FROM THE BALL SHOULD BE PRECISE

This is closely related to posture and knee flex, so let's talk about it here. Standing the correct distance from the ball at address is vital if I am to make a sound swing. If I'm too close or too far away, I'm forced to make all sorts of anatomical adjustments in order to compensate—and I won't compensate very well.

Top Left—I'm Standing Too Close: This forces my knees into that locked position we talked about. What's more, my spine is too upright. My arms don't have room to swing freely, I can't turn my shoulders on the correct plane, and I'm destined to swing the club way too upright going back and coming down. The ball can go anywhere from this position, and you can bet it won't go very far.

Bottom Left—I'm Too Far Away: This is a horrible position. To reach the ball, I have to extend my arms out from my body. I'm bent over too much at the waist and my knees show too much flex. The tendency is to lift the spine on the backswing and then pitch forward on the downswing. The ball is bound to go anywhere but straight.

Opposite Page—I'm "Measured Off" Just Right: The signs that I'm standing the correct distance from the ball are clear. My arms are hanging comfortably, just a shade outside of vertical. My knees are flexed ever so slightly, I'm bent over at the hips comfortably but not too far, and my weight is evenly distributed between my heels and toes. Now I can turn back and through the ball without changing my spine angle or my knee flex. When I swing, my arms, hands and club have a great chance of returning to the position I've established at address.

BEGINNING THE BACKSWING

Now the real fun is about to begin. Let's start the full swing by setting the club into motion correctly. Notice I said the club, not your body. The reason you've worked hard at positioning your body the right way is so it can transport the club on the proper path and plane throughout the swing.

Start the Club "On Line"

Midway through the backswing, the club should be parallel with your stance line. You get it there by swinging the club back with your shoulders, arms and hands working together smoothly. From here, it's easy to swing the club into perfect position at the top of the backswing.

Don't Let the Club Stray Inside

I've made this mistake many times, and it's a killer. If the club moves too far to the inside midway through the backswing, the shaft aiming to the right of my target, I'm forced to make compensations (I call them "makeup moves") to get the club back on the right track. If I return the club to this position on the down-swing, I'll probably push the ball to the right.

SIX KEYS TO A GREAT BACKSWING

H ere are six checkpoints to ensure you've arrived at a great position at the top of the swing.

■ I let my right elbow come away from my side, but I make sure it points toward the ground.

■ My left shoulder should be turned under my chin. That's easier to do if I keep my chin held high throughout the swing.

■ I keep my right knee flexed, the same way I had it at address.

■ My clubface should be "square" at the top, meaning it is parallel to my left forearm.

■ My left heel stays flat on the ground, which helps restrict my hip turn, creating more torque.

■ My weight is gathered onto my right heel.

PRACTICE MAKES PERMANENT

Most golfers encounter streaks where their swing falls into place and they play very well for a short period of time. On the other hand, they fall into slumps where the swing doesn't feel right and the ball goes everywhere except where they're aiming.

My goal—and it may be unattainable—is to groove my swing to the extent that I play my best golf all the time. There is only one way that's going to happen: Practice and more practice. Long ago, I committed myself to the idea that there are no shortcuts to improvement. The best way to ingrain the correct movements and positions is through repetition.

Some players look at practice as drudgery. I happen to love it. Give me a big pile of balls, a new glove, my clubs and some nice turf, and I'm one happy human. Other golfers may outplay me from time to time, but they'll never outwork me.

IN SEARCH OF THE "SLOT"

I talked about positioning the club correctly midway through the backswing. The reason I stress that so much is because you then have a much better chance of setting it in that elusive position known as the "slot" at the top of the swing. Check your reflection in the mirror or a window to see where your club is, then work on setting it correctly.

I've Found the "Slot"

This is the ideal top-of-backswing position. The shaft is parallel to the target line, just as it was midway through the backswing. If I start the downswing by shifting my lower body to the left and unturning my hips, the club will drop down and approach the ball on the perfect path and plane.

The Club Is "Laid Off"
If the club points to the left of the target at the top, you are prone to "coming over the top" on the downswing. You'll cut across the ball from out to in and hit a slice or pull.

The Club Is "Across the Line"
If the club points to the right of the target at the top, you are "across the line" and will likely swing the club down too much from the inside. That means a block to the right or a big hook.

THE CLUB FEELS HEAVIER THAN IT SHOULD AND OUT OF BALANCE TOO.

FROM HERE, THE CLUB MUST FOLLOW A COMPLICATED ROUTE TO IMPACT.

LET GRAVITY RULE

The faster you swing the club through impact, the farther the ball goes. That's a simple equation, but obtaining speed and power on the downswing is easier said than done. A problem almost every golfer encounters is rushing the down-swing—letting loose with every-thing you have the moment the backswing is complete. When you do that, however, nothing works in proper sequence. The shoulders outrace the arms, the arms outrace the hands and the hands outrace the club. All that speed is expended too soon and the clubhead is actually losing speed as it strikes the ball, when it should be accelerating.

I like to start the downswing by shifting my weight easily back to my left side, and then letting my arms "fall" downward in front of my chest. I don't want my shoulders unwinding so fast that they get way ahead of my arms. By giving my arms a little head start, they work in concert with my shoulders to create a real package of power coming into the ball. That good timing allows me to hit the ball a mile, and I don't have to try very hard to do it.

5
HOW TO FLAG YOUR IRONS

KNOCKING DOWN THE PIN

All things considered, it's easier to play golf during the day than at night. I learned that as a kid when my dad and I used to sneak out on a military golf course near our home and play a few holes just as darkness was gathering. And I learned it all over again at Firestone Country Club in the final round of the 2000 NEC Invitational. I had a substantial lead coming up the 18th hole, and it was so dark people up by the green were holding up cigarette lighters as if it were a rock concert. There had been a three-hour rain delay earlier in the day, and now it was so black I could barely make out the flagstick on the green.

My ball, from what I could see of it, was sitting up pretty well in the first cut of rough. I had 168 yards to the pin. The one thing I didn't want to do was hit an absolutely terrible shot that would lead to a double bogey or something. True, I had a big lead, but I wanted to close things out in style.

I chose an 8-iron and made a couple of practice swings, just to feel where the ground was in relation to the clubhead. I could tell the turf was very firm and felt I'd be able to deliver the ball my normal 8-iron distance. Then I got over the ball, swung and hoped for the best. I saw the ball take off, but then lost it in the darkness about 30 yards into its flight. The next thing I heard was a huge roar from the gallery up by the green. My ball had come to rest two feet from the hole, and the birdie gave me the kind of victory I was looking for.

Looking back, I suppose I could have used a pitching wedge and played the ball just short of the green, to avoid the bunkers and any real trouble. But whenever I get an iron in my hands, my first instinct is to be aggressive. The irons are the true offensive weapons in golf. I always feel a surge of excitement just pulling an iron from the bag, because that's where the process of making birdies really begins. If you're capable of hitting the ball close to the hole, you're capable of shooting low scores.

BUILDING A STABLE BASE

On every shot, you need a combination of balance, stability and ease of movement. Those factors are largely determined by stance width—how far apart you position your feet at address. Stance width is especially important with your irons, as they are precision clubs that demand a rock-solid base with your lower body.

▲ *The Driver and Woods from the Fairway:* My feet are spread wide to accommodate my big shoulder turn and fast upper-body movement during the swing. A narrower stance would encourage a sway; a wider stance would limit my weight shift.

▲ *Short Shots:* My swing with the short irons isn't super long, and I rarely swing with all my effort. Therefore, I don't need a wide base. When I'm pitching or chipping, my stance is narrower still.

◄ *The 5-iron:* As the club becomes shorter, my stance width becomes narrower. My stance is wide enough to allow me to keep my balance, but not so far apart that it restricts motion in my upper body. With each club, it is important to be consistent with my stance width on every shot. That is the only way to produce consistent results.

Three things happen when I choke down on my irons: I hit the ball a bit straighter, I get a lower ball flight, and the ball doesn't check up as quickly when it hits the green.

CHOKE GASP!

THERE'S NO STOPPING
THIS BACKSWING.

KEEP YOUR CHIN UP

· · · · · · · · · · · · · · · · · · ·

Good posture is important on every shot. At address I make sure my back is fairly straight and that I have a bit of flex in my knees. My body is now prepared to move freely in any direction during the swing.

One of the most important aspects of good posture is to hold your chin high at address. It's something Butch Harmon and I check constantly. You want your chin well off your chest so your left shoulder has plenty of room to turn under your chin on the backswing. This is one of my key thoughts.

The Finished Product

As you can see, my shoulders are turning freely with no interference from my chin. This wasn't always the case. I used to stand too close to the ball, which caused me to lower my chin just to see the ball clearly when I looked down at address. I sometimes felt crowded, and no wonder—there was very little room for my shoulders to turn and my arms to swing. Today I stand farther from the ball, with my head held high throughout the swing. My change in posture allows me to turn freely, back and through.

A 9-iron shot won't hook or slice as much as a 5-iron shot. The more loft you have, the less sidespin you can impart on the ball.

THINK "WIDE" ON THE BACKSWING

The proper backswing is a combination of horizontal and vertical movement. Most amateurs err on the vertical side—they start the swing by lifting the arms straight up and cocking the wrists immediately. Because the backswing is too vertical, the downswing is too vertical as well. The tendency is to chop down on the ball instead of swinging through it smoothly.

Don't forget the "horizontal" part of the backswing. That means establishing a nice, wide swing arc as soon as you move the club back. I have the feeling of stretching my hands and arms away from my body early in the backswing, my wrists beginning to cock naturally after the clubhead reaches about knee height. That helps me accumulate power and also ensures that my downswing won't be too steep.

A Bad Start

The takeaway I'm modeling here is too steep and vertical. The arc of my swing is narrow already, and by the time I get to the top of the swing it will be too late to widen it. You can bet the downswing will be too steep, too. That means deep divots, fat shots and an inconsistent ball flight.

NO
A TIGHT, NARROW, STEEP BACKSWING.

YES

**HOW FAR FROM MY
HEAD CAN I MOVE
MY HANDS?**

I UNIFY MY BACKSWING

I believe in a nice, wide backswing, but I don't like a backswing that is too loose. I don't want my arms running away from my upper body. That would lead to a "fake backswing"—the club reaching parallel, but only due to excessive wrist-cocking or the arms swinging back too far. That leads to a weak downswing in which you slap at the ball with your hands and arms alone.

I try to swing the club back with everything—hips, shoulders, arms and hands—working together. When I turn my shoulders fully, they accommodate the swinging of my arms to create a strong, unified package at the top of the backswing.

Tighten That Turn
One way to prevent your arms from out-racing your upper body is to check the position of your right arm at various stages of the backswing. When Butch and I work together, he checks that my right arm is kept fairly close to my side and in front of my torso as I complete my shoulder turn. I don't like my arms to feel cramped, but I don't want them straying too far from my body, either.

MY SHOULDERS AND
ARMS TRANSPORT THE
CLUB TOGETHER.

START DOWN SLOW

When good players talk about "getting too quick," they're almost always talking about the first move down from the top of the backswing. The beginning of the downswing can't be rushed. You want your swing to gather speed gradually, so that everything works in sequence and the clubhead reaches its maximum speed at impact. If you start down suddenly, all your speed and power are gone by the time you reach impact. Your timing and mechanics are shot, too.

Remember, there can only be one fast moment in the swing, and it had better be when the club strikes the ball.

SLOW TO HERE,
THEN POUR ON
THE POWER.

DOWN AND THROUGH

. . . .

One of the keys to good ball striking is to hit *through* the ball, not at it. In my mind, the ball is merely an object that is in the way of the clubhead as it tears through the hitting area. I don't try to end my swing abruptly after the ball is struck. I try to keep the clubhead accelerating down the target line as long as I comfortably can.

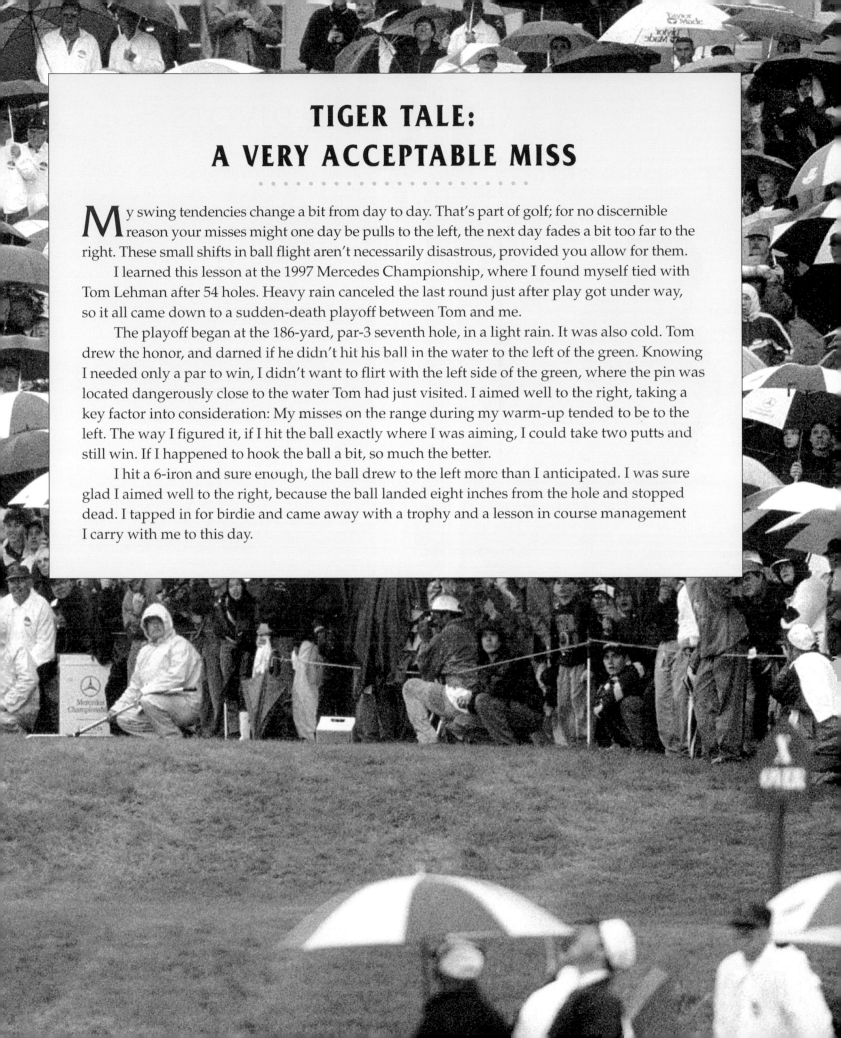

TIGER TALE:
A VERY ACCEPTABLE MISS

M y swing tendencies change a bit from day to day. That's part of golf; for no discernible reason your misses might one day be pulls to the left, the next day fades a bit too far to the right. These small shifts in ball flight aren't necessarily disastrous, provided you allow for them.

I learned this lesson at the 1997 Mercedes Championship, where I found myself tied with Tom Lehman after 54 holes. Heavy rain canceled the last round just after play got under way, so it all came down to a sudden-death playoff between Tom and me.

The playoff began at the 186-yard, par-3 seventh hole, in a light rain. It was also cold. Tom drew the honor, and darned if he didn't hit his ball in the water to the left of the green. Knowing I needed only a par to win, I didn't want to flirt with the left side of the green, where the pin was located dangerously close to the water Tom had just visited. I aimed well to the right, taking a key factor into consideration: My misses on the range during my warm-up tended to be to the left. The way I figured it, if I hit the ball exactly where I was aiming, I could take two putts and still win. If I happened to hook the ball a bit, so much the better.

I hit a 6-iron and sure enough, the ball drew to the left more than I anticipated. I was sure glad I aimed well to the right, because the ball landed eight inches from the hole and stopped dead. I tapped in for birdie and came away with a trophy and a lesson in course management I carry with me to this day.

A TALE OF TWO DIVOTS

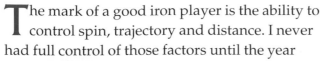

The mark of a good iron player is the ability to control spin, trajectory and distance. I never had full control of those factors until the year following my victory in the 1997 Masters. Only after a long period of hard work was I able to get my iron play where I wanted it. One of the swing changes I made altered the look of my divots, especially with my short and middle irons. Prior to 1997, I took deep, heavy divots that sometimes were as big as dinner plates. The divots may have looked cool flying through the air, but they showed my downswing was too steep and that I was delofting the clubface through impact. As a result I couldn't adjust the ball's spin, trajectory or distance worth a darn. The swing change I made shallowed out my swing so the clubhead approached the ball at an angle that was closer to level.

The divots I took after the swing change looked a lot different. Instead of being long and deep, they were long and shallow, about the size of a dollar bill. I can still take a big divot when I have to, but the standard divot should be long and thin.

THIS IS THE LOOK OF A PERFECT DIVOT.

THIS DIVOT IS TOO BIG!

More Causes of Deep Divots

There are other reasons why divots can be deep and irregular. It may be that your ball is positioned too far back in your stance, which necessitates a steep angle of approach with the clubhead. You may be throwing the clubhead at the ball with your arms and hands alone, instead of assisting with your shoulders. Or you may be "coming over the top" on the downswing, in which case the gash made by your divot points well to the left of your target line.

A SWEET FINISH

The look of my follow-through serves as sort of a road map for what happened earlier in my swing. See how my arms are extended? That shows my swing was real wide, with good extension through the ball. See how far my shoulders have unwound? That shows my swing was predicated on a full shoulder turn instead of just my hands and arms. Finally, see how the toe of the club points straight down? That proves I didn't rotate the club excessively with my hands through impact. For it to arrive at this position, I had to release the club naturally.

MY TEEING HEIGHT
FOR A LONG IRON.

THE ART OF TEEING THE BALL

. . . .

When playing a par-3 hole, the first rule is to always use a tee. As my hero Jack Nicklaus once said, "I found out a long time ago that air offers less resistance than dirt." Using a tee goes a long way to guaranteeing solid contact.

How high you tee the ball depends on the club you're hitting and how much spin you want to put on the ball. With long irons, I tee the ball about half an inch high. That's pretty far off the

ground, but because I'm sweeping the ball off the tee, there's little chance I'll catch the ball too high on the clubface. My thought as I sweep through the ball is to clip the tops of the grass, leaving the tee in the ground.

With the more-lofted clubs like the 7- to 9-irons, I tee the ball much lower, barely above the turf. My swing naturally gets more upright as the loft of the club increases, so I'm hitting down on the ball more.

I THINK, THEN I SWING

Most of the amateurs I play with adopt one of two strategies for their approach shots: They either aim for the green in general, hoping they'll wind up with a putt for birdie. That strategy is much too broad. Or they aim for the flagstick every time without giving much thought to the consequences of an errant shot. That strategy is too one-dimensional.

I always aim for a specific part of the green, which may or may not be right next to the hole. I take into consideration the kind of putt I'll face from various spots on the green, and respect the trouble that will result if the shot doesn't come off

as planned. This strategy has served me well throughout my career, especially on courses such as Augusta National, where the tricky greens often dictate that I play to a spot 20 feet or more from the hole.

The point is, don't just grab a club and let it rip. Good iron play is as much about course management and smart strategy as it is about executing the swing. Think before you leap, and you won't make big numbers.

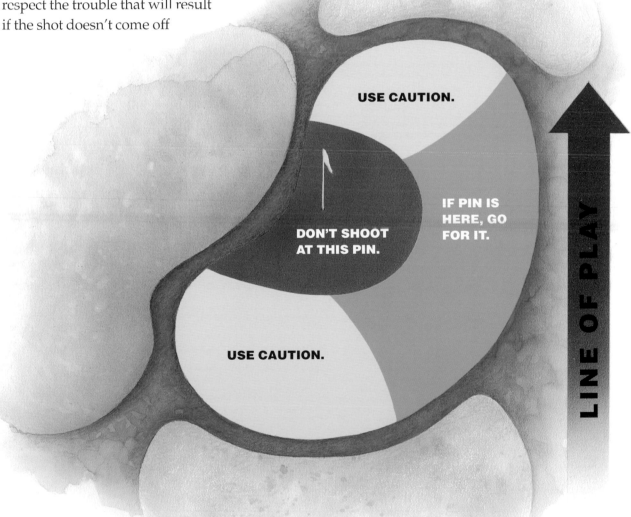

USE CAUTION.

DON'T SHOOT AT THIS PIN.

IF PIN IS HERE, GO FOR IT.

USE CAUTION.

LINE OF PLAY

HOW I HIT THE 2-IRON STINGER

. . . .

In 1998, Butch Harmon and I began working on a specialty shot with my 2-iron. I call it my "stinger," because it bores through the wind beautifully and rolls up to 80 yards. I tee the ball low and play it back in my stance, with my hands set well ahead. I also flex my knees more than usual.

I turn my shoulders fully going back, maintaining that flex in my knees. I start the downswing deliberately, keeping my hands and arms in front of my chest. I hit down firmly. However, I make sure my downswing isn't too steep. I accelerate through the ball, but maintain my balance. For accuracy's sake, I extend the clubhead straight down the target line after impact. My follow-through is a bit shorter than with the other clubs.

Please turn the page →

EQUIPPED FOR SUCCESS

People ask me all the time if they can look at my clubs. They are curious about my set makeup as well as the type of weapons I carry. I can tell you, I play thin-bladed forged irons, which aren't forgiving at all. I love them—they provide wonderful feedback and feel. But I've practiced many hours to learn to play these kinds of clubs. Most amateurs, however, would be better served by some kind of sole-heavy, cavity-back design, which delivers good results on off-center hits and helps them get the ball in the air.

You'll notice I carry the 2- and 3-irons. Unless you're a 4-handicap player or less who generates a lot of club-head speed, the long irons aren't such a hot idea either. They're too demanding and you wouldn't use them more than once or twice a round anyway. I suggest you give some lofted utility woods (a 5- and 7-wood) a try. They're much more versatile and will save you a lot of strokes.

One thing we should have in common is more than one sand wedge.

A single sand wedge just doesn't cut it anymore. Add a lob wedge (something with about 60 degrees of loft) and you'll save par more often.

MY EQUIPMENT IS FAIRLY TRADITIONAL.

FINISHING THOUGHTS

. . . .

One of the secrets to good iron play is to keep things simple. The number of situations I encounter may be endless, but the same sound, no-frills swing is sufficient to deal with almost all of them. Let's review my fundamental keys to hitting the irons solidly and consistently.

■ The longer the iron, the farther forward I position the ball in my stance.

■ I sweep the longer irons, hit down on the rest. I trust the club's loft to get the ball airborne.

■ My backswing with the irons is shorter than with the woods.

■ To promote good timing, I start down slowly from the top of the backswing.

■ The clubhead strikes the ball first, the turf last. I don't begin to take a divot until the ball has left the clubface.

■ I swing within myself. On standard shots, I never expend more than 80 percent of my effort.

■ The worse my lie, the farther back I position my ball in my stance.

■ I always tee my ball on par 3s. You want every edge you can get.

■ The perfect divot is about the same size and shape as a dollar bill.

❖6❖
HOW TO NAIL FAIRWAY WOODS

PLAYING THE VERSATILE CLUBS

Whereas a lot of golfers use the 3-wood almost exclusively from the fairway, I tend to use mine mainly from the tee. Because distance isn't a problem for me, I often go with the 3-wood instead of the driver just to keep the ball in play. But sometimes, when I'm playing a monster par 5 that is almost unreachable in two, I'll go for the green with my 3-wood, hoping to attain as much distance as possible while also exerting some degree of control and precision. The best example of this type of shot is the 3-wood I played on the 18th hole at Pebble Beach in the final round of the 1998 AT&T Pebble Beach National Pro-Am.

Coming to the last hole I was trailing my good friend and neighbor, Mark O'Meara, by two strokes. Mark was playing just behind me, and I knew I probably needed an eagle to have a chance. A good drive left me with 267 yards to the front of the green, just inside the first cut of rough. Fortunately for me, the PGA Tour had applied the lift, clean and place rule due to heavy rains earlier in the week. So I placed my ball in a perfect cupcake lie just into the first cut of rough. I was licking my chops just waiting to get at it.

The shot itself wasn't so easy. It was cold and the wind was blowing into my face and slightly from right to left, toward the water that guards the left side of the fairway and green. Now, when the wind is blowing from the right, I usually elect to fade the ball so it's curving into the wind. But to reach the green, I had to play a powerful draw.

I aimed at the edge of the grandstand to the right of the green, got set, then swung as hard as I possibly could. I smoked it. The shot came off just as I saw it in my mind's eye, drawing beautifully and reaching the front of the green. I didn't make the putt for eagle, and the tap-in birdie wasn't enough to catch Mark. But that shot affirmed what I knew deep inside: That I could attempt a difficult shot under pressure with everything on the line, and actually pull it off.

ADDRESS: ACT NATURALLY

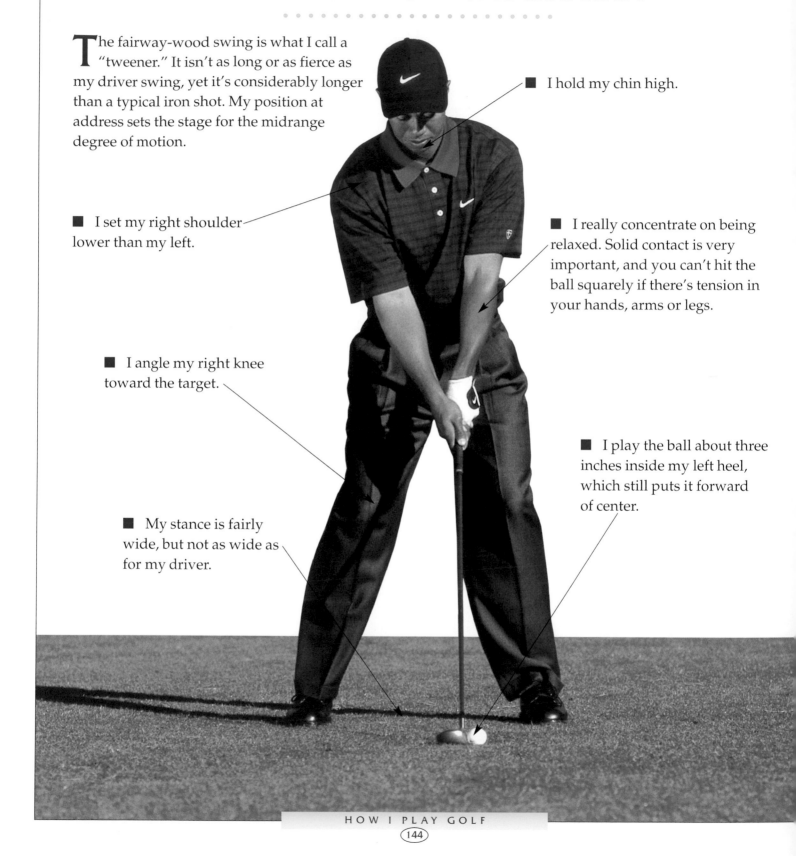

The fairway-wood swing is what I call a "tweener." It isn't as long or as fierce as my driver swing, yet it's considerably longer than a typical iron shot. My position at address sets the stage for the midrange degree of motion.

■ I hold my chin high.

■ I set my right shoulder lower than my left.

■ I really concentrate on being relaxed. Solid contact is very important, and you can't hit the ball squarely if there's tension in your hands, arms or legs.

■ I angle my right knee toward the target.

■ I play the ball about three inches inside my left heel, which still puts it forward of center.

■ My stance is fairly wide, but not as wide as for my driver.

SWEEP BACK TO SWEEP THROUGH

. . . .

I like to sweep the ball cleanly off the turf with the clubhead moving absolutely level with the ground at the moment of impact. I don't like to pinch the ball off the turf, and I sure as heck don't want to hit up on the ball as I do with my driver. To encourage this level angle of approach, I take the clubhead away from the ball in the same manner I want it to swing through on the downswing—low to the ground with a nice, wide arc. This not only promotes the right swing path and angle of approach, it establishes good tempo and smooth rhythm.

From light rough, you'll find a fairway wood is much easier to hit than a long iron.

AT THE TOP OF THE BACK-SWING, YOU WANT TO FEEL RELAXED YET POISED.

AT THE TOP: EASY DOES IT

Although the fairway wood shot is designed to crank the ball out there a long way, I don't like to sacrifice a millimeter of accuracy. I keep my swing very controlled. I don't lengthen my swing unnecessarily and I take special care not to let tension creep into any part of my body.

Look closely, and you can see how the fairway wood swing differs from my driver swing. Note that both my feet are planted firmly on the ground. Although I allow my hips to turn, my lower body is quieter than with the driver. See how I allow my left arm to bend a little at the elbow? By keeping it soft and supple, I can generate plenty of speed while preserving touch and control. My clubshaft is short of parallel, too. I turn my shoulders quite a bit, but I don't want the club to get away from me so my hands are quiet at the top.

I'M FULLY COILED,
BUT THERE'S NO
SENSE OF STRAIN.

DON'T MISS YOUR PLANE

Swinging the club down on the ideal swing plane is important with every club in the bag, but it's especially crucial with fairway woods. Midway into my downswing, I like to see my clubshaft aligned perfectly with the ball. If the club were more vertical at this point, my downswing would be too steep. If the club were more flat or horizontal, I'd have to spin my lower body frantically in order to hit the ball solidly.

When the clubshaft is on plane, two good things happen. The club feels light and balanced, making it easy to generate all the clubhead speed I need. More important, there is little chance of hitting a big slice or hook because the clubshaft is all but trapped within that perfect little channel I've created. From here, it's actually easier to hit a good shot than a bad one. That's a satisfying feeling that produces confidence.

WHEN I'M ON PLANE AT THIS POINT, THE REST OF THE DOWNSWING IS A PIECE OF CAKE.

THE STYLE SHOULD SUIT THE PLAYER

UTILITY WOOD

HIGH-LOFTED FAIRWAY WOOD

3-WOOD

You should experiment with several types of fairway woods before deciding which models to include in your set. Before considering loft, lie and shaft flex, you first need to determine which basic clubhead design will serve you best.

Utility Value
This type of utility fairway wood is very popular among amateurs, and you'll even find a few on the Senior PGA Tour. The clubface is shallow with most of the weight distributed along the bottom of the clubhead to hit the ball higher and advance the ball from tall grass.

Just Right for the Average Joe
This type of fairway wood is useful for the everyday amateur. The head is oversized, with a big, forgiving sweet spot. It's easy to get the ball airborne, but is also useful off the tee on a short, tight par 4 or a long par 3. It complements the utility wood very well; most amateurs should carry this model *and* a utility wood as well.

Don't Try This at Home
My 3-wood—the only fairway wood I carry, incidentally—is similar to this one in terms of design. The clubhead is medium-sized, the weight distributed fairly evenly around the perimeter and from top to bottom. It gives me exceptional feel and control, but you need a lot of clubhead speed and have to nail the sweet spot to get much out of it. Not a great club to hit from poor lies—if the ball is sitting badly I'll use an iron.

MY POSITION AT ADDRESS IS
A SNEAK PREVIEW OF WHERE
I WANT TO BE AT IMPACT.

IMPACT SHOULD LOOK LIKE ADDRESS

The purpose of addressing the ball correctly is so you can return to that position at impact. These photos aren't spitting images, of course—in the photo at left I'm absolutely still while in the photo at right I'm set to launch the ball at 180 m.p.h.—but they are more alike than they are different. You'll note that the clubshaft is in almost exactly the same position in both photos, perpendicular to the target line. My spine angle is the same and my head is in virtually the same spot. It proves how uncomplicated the golf swing can be.

The differences can be attributed to speed and motion. My hips and shoulders are rotating furiously in the photo at right and thus are a bit open to the target line. My arms are farther forward because they are swinging past my body with as much speed as I can muster. And my right heel is off the ground (though you can't see it well here) to accommodate the movement in my hips and shoulders.

So, while I've arrived at a pretty good position at impact, the big lesson here is to set up to the ball in a manner that allows you to swing the club freely with no unnecessary movement in any part of your body.

A "BORING" PROPOSITION

I'm a big believer in the importance of trajectory and ball flight. Because the fairway woods can have considerable loft, it's all too easy to settle for a high, lazy ball flight. That isn't my style. I like the ball to come off the clubface with lots of zip, so it can bore through the wind without being blown off line too much. I like to hear the ball hiss for the first 30 yards or so.

A boring ball flight is not just a product of hitting the ball hard. Much of it has to do with the clubhead's angle of attack, how solidly you hit the ball and the type of fairway wood you're using. You'll get more out of your fairway woods if you can achieve: (1) a level angle of attack into the ball; (2) center-face contact; and (3) a fairway wood that is properly fitted to your swing in terms of weight, shaft flex and clubhead design. Once you find the right fairway wood, you'll find the search was well worth the effort.

THE FEELING HERE IS ONE OF THROWING THE CLUBHEAD DOWN THE LINE WITH MY RIGHT HAND.

"CHASE" THE BALL WITH YOUR RIGHT HAND

On second shots into long par 4s and short par 5s, you're aiming at a pretty small target. Accuracy is extremely important and not all that easy to achieve. Keep in mind, the fairway wood is a lot longer than, say, your 7-iron and thus is harder to control. The best key for keeping the ball on the straight and narrow is to make the clubhead track straight down the target line for as long as possible after impact. You should feel you are chasing the ball into the distance with your right hand, keeping the clubhead low to the ground and allowing your right arm to extend fully after it has struck the ball. This will keep the clubface square to the target for a longer period through impact.

WHEN I MUST TURN THE BALL LEFT

Only after years of practice am I able to shape my tee shots at will without changing the basic character of my swing. The benefit of all this work led to my winning my sixth professional major, and the fourth in a row, the 2001 Masters. The 13th hole at Augusta National is a par 5 that bends sharply to the left about 230 yards out from the tee. The player who can hit a long, controlled draw on demand has a big advantage there, for once the ball turns the corner, it can scamper to within 200 yards of the green. And because of the elusive nature of the firm, undulating green, it's a treat to have a middle iron in your hand to use on your approach shot.

Long before I arrived at Augusta for the 2001 Masters, I practiced that draw with my driver and 3-wood. For two months solid, I would devote a little extra time on the practice tee with that specific shot in my mind's eye. I don't consciously change my mechanics. I do it by feel. My last thought before I take the club back is "Draw." I got good at hitting the shot in practice, but would it hold up under pressure?

I found out in the final round. Nursing a narrow lead over Phil Mickelson and David Duval, I stood on the 13th tee determined to bring off that hard, piercing draw. Filled with the confidence that comes from knowing you've prepared yourself well, I grabbed my 3-wood and just ripped the tee shot. The ball not only turned the corner, it didn't stop rolling until it came to rest in a perfect lie, 183 yards from the green. I hit the green easily, and the tap-in birdie that followed kept my lead intact—a lead, as it turned out, I wouldn't lose.

❖ 7 ❖
HOW TO SMOKE THE DRIVER

GOING WITH ALL YOU'VE GOT

If one club in my bag qualifies as being more important than any other, it's the driver. A lot of people will tell you it's the putter simply because more strokes are made with the flat stick during a round than with any other club. But the driver gets my vote for several reasons. A good drive makes all things possible. My chances of making a birdie or eagle are increased enormously when I crush the ball long and straight. What's more, if my swing with the driver is sound, my swing with the irons tends to be good as well. As the driver goes, so goes the rest of my game from tee to green.

But the biggest thing about the driver isn't tactical or mechanical. To me, the driver has the special capability of giving me an emotional lift and a big edge psychologically. A super drive that stops on the center mowing stripe fills me with strength, energy and confidence.

Nowhere was the emotional lift from a good drive more apparent—or more necessary—than on the final hole of the 2001 Masters. I came to the 18th tee knowing I had the tournament sewn up—provided I made a par 4. A bogey would put me in a playoff against David Duval. This was not a time to play defensively. I chose the driver and committed myself to ripping the ball almost as hard as I could. I set up to play a fade, and swung as aggressively as I had all week.

Television viewers saw me hold my finish extra long, and they might have thought I was just enjoying the moment, but I was trying to watch my ball finish. It literally went out of my sight. I thought I might have faded the ball too much around the corner of the dogleg, that it could have drifted into the trees on the right. As I walked up the fairway, I saw a ball sitting in the right rough, but it was Phil Mickelson's, not mine. I looked farther up ahead, and lo and behold, there was my ball, sitting pretty in the fairway, only 78 yards from the green. Man, was I relieved—and excited. The little wedge shot I had left was nothing, and one putt later, I had my second green jacket and fourth straight major championship.

A FOUNDATION FOR POWER

. . . .

My stance is wider with the driver than for any other club. That's because my driver swing is longer, wider and (on the downswing at least) a lot faster. Spreading my feet slightly wider than my shoulders gives me the stability I need to really go after it. I flex my knees just a little, enough to make them feel alive and promote easy movement in my trunk and torso.

I also pay close attention to my foot position at address. I've found that by flaring my right foot out to my right ever so slightly, I'm able to make a modest hip turn without straining my knee and thigh. As for my left foot, I flare it out slightly in the opposite direction, toward the target. This prevents me from turning my hips too far on the backswing, and allows me to rotate my upper body freely on the downswing and into my follow-through without putting too much pressure on my leg and back.

Finally, I like to angle my knee inward just a bit at address. That encourages me to turn rather than slide on the backswing, and makes it easier to shift my weight to the left on the downswing.

Extra Width for Extra Distance
When I'm playing a par 5 that is reachable in two and the fairway is fairly wide, I sometimes will swing as hard as I can. When I plan to go all out with the driver, I spread my feet even wider than normal. That gives me a firmer base so I won't lose my balance. What's more, a wider stance helps me station most of my weight on my right side. One of the keys to distance is keeping the upper body to the right of the ball on the downswing, and a wider stance helps me do that. The wider the stance, the more difficult it is to sway laterally on the forward swing.

A WELL-BUILT HOUSE IS WIDEST AT THE FOUNDATION. THE SAME GOES FOR MY SETUP— MY FEET ARE WIDER THAN MY SHOULDERS.

WIDER

A POWERFUL START

The sequence of motion on the backswing is the same for the driver as for every other club. But I do pay special attention to my hips. I make absolutely sure that my hips turn rather than slide to my right. Turning the hips is one of the first signs I'm accumulating power. This rotary motion in my hips and shoulders is much like loading a giant spring. By the time I reach the top, my hips and shoulders are primed to unload with tremendous speed.

HIPS SLIDE— A KILLER FAULT.

HIPS TURN NICELY.

The Most Common Backswing Error
Shifting your hips laterally to the right just kills your backswing. If your right hip moves outside of your right foot, you have to slide back to the left just to hit the ball. It's hard to time that move properly. What's more, you've cut your power by about 50 percent, because a sliding motion on the

downswing isn't anywhere near as powerful as a rotary unwinding of the hips and shoulders. A good thought is to keep your weight on the inside portion of your right foot, keeping the angle of your right leg constant throughout the backswing. This is something I've worked on since I was a kid; it is an absolute trademark of my swing.

I START MY SWING SLOWLY AND
SMOOTHLY, SETTING THE STAGE
FOR WHAT YOU SEE ON THE
FOLLOWING PAGES.

WHEN ALL GOES RIGHT,
I ARRIVE AT THE FINISH
YOU SEE HERE.

THINK "LONG AND WIDE"

I have two goals on my takeaway: To establish a very wide swing arc, and to shift my weight fully to my right side without sliding to my right. I try to extend the butt end of the shaft as far from my right hip as I possibly can, my shoulders turning to make it possible. You'll notice that my right leg is angled toward the target a bit even though I've clearly shifted my weight onto my right side.

MY SHOULDERS TURN FARTHER THAN MY HIPS

With the driver, I turn my shoulders as far as they'll go. My hips turn, too, but my shoulders turn a lot farther. There should be a healthy feeling of tension and resistance down your left side at the top. From here, all I have to do is unwind my hips a bit, and my shoulders will follow, unturning with tremendous speed on the downswing.

When I'm driving downwind I often leave the driver in the bag and go with my 3-wood. I carry the ball just as far, and increase my chances of hitting the ball straight.

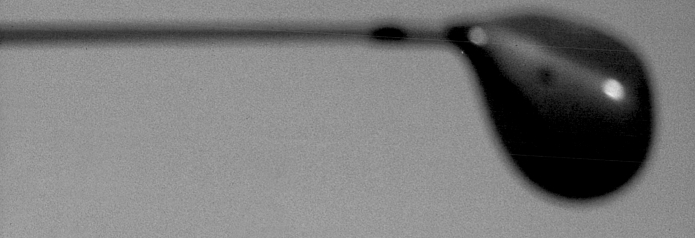

I TURN MY LEFT SHOULDER UNDER MY CHIN

· · · · · · · · · · · · · · · · · · · ·

I know I'm making a full shoulder turn when my left shoulder turns under my chin. I try to turn my shoulders at least 90 degrees from their position at address, enough so my left shoulder is well behind the ball at the top. Butch Harmon tells me that Ben Hogan used to wear out his shirts at the point where the left shoulder moved under the chin.

A full shoulder turn means I don't have to force the issue on the downswing. My shoulders will unwind fast but smoothly, carrying the arms along with them on their powerful route to impact.

TIGER TALE:
DRIVING WITH DISTRACTION

· ·

T he driver swing is the most physical act in all of golf. But there's a strong mental aspect to it, too. To consistently drive the ball long and straight, you need to be single-minded about what you're doing. You must be totally impervious to distractions and immune to thoughts that can make your swing fall to pieces. Because the driver swing is long and a bit violent in terms of the sheer speed you're trying to generate, timing is extremely important. If you allow something to break your concentration and upset your rhythm or tempo, you're in deep trouble.

Staying focused can be a tall order for me, simply because there are large numbers of people very close by on virtually every drive I hit.

The gallery grows so quiet when I'm preparing to hit that when someone does speak or a camera clicks, it can sound like a bomb going off. My goal is to be so focused that I don't hear these disruptions—or at least don't allow them to influence my swing.

In the final round of the 2001 Masters, I arrived at the 15th tee doing my best to protect a fragile one-stroke lead over David Duval. The drive on the 15th, a reachable par 5, is critical. A long, accurate tee shot sets up a middle-iron approach over water to a firm, sloping green. You really need a birdie there to avoid giving a shot back to the field. This was on my mind as I conducted my preshot routine then set up over the ball.

I made a nice, full backswing and made my first move down from the top, the club dropping right into the "slot." Then, out of nowhere, a camera clicked. Startled badly, I somehow managed to stop my downswing before the club hit the ball. And I'm glad I did, or I might not have gotten that second green jacket.

It goes to show that good driving is partly the result of having good concentration and presence of mind. I was focused on what I was doing that day, yet somehow aware of my surroundings. If I can manage myself with a couple of hundred people within whispering distance, you can learn to do it on Saturday mornings with only a couple of buddies nearby.

IT'S COOL TO BE SQUARE

The position you establish at the top serves as a preview of where you'll be at impact. One of my goals is to achieve a "square" clubface at the top of the backswing, meaning it should be parallel with my left forearm. If the toe of the clubhead were pointing more toward the ground, my clubface would be open and I'd tend to hit a big slice. If the clubface were aimed dead at the sky, the clubface would be closed and I'd lean toward hitting a big hook.

KEEP CLUB SHORT OF PARALLEL

I believe in a big shoulder turn, but I don't like the club dipping past parallel with the ground. Actually, the shoulders aren't to blame for the club going back too far. It happens because the left arm bends too much at the elbow or the hands don't maintain a firm hold on the club. When the shaft extends beyond parallel, you tend to "throw" the club from the top with the hands, rather than letting the unturning of the shoulders transport the club into a sound position on the downswing.

LOWER BODY LEADS THE WAY

On the downswing, the sequence of motion is from the ground up. First you shift your weight to your left leg, then you turn your hips with all you've got. The shoulders come next; as you can see in the photo, my shoulders are still square to the target even though my hips are aligned well to the left. The arms and hands come last. If you've performed everything in order, they'll deliver the clubhead into the ball along the correct inside path.

Remember, the chain of events occurs slowly at first. If you rush, you'll likely unwind your shoulders too soon and perform the dreaded "over the top" move, where the club is delivered into the ball on an out-to-in path. That means a loss of power and, more than likely, a big slice to the right.

FOR MORE YARDS, I "SNAP" MY LEFT LEG

When I need an extra 20 yards, I incorporate a special move in my lower body just before impact. I've found that by snapping my left leg straight, my hips clear faster and speed up the movement of my shoulders, arms and legs. This is an unorthodox move meant solely for power. Byron Nelson and many other great ball strikers concentrate on maintaining a bit of flex in their left leg through impact, as that tends to keep the clubhead moving along the target line longer. But for extra distance, I straighten that left leg as quickly as I can on the through-swing.

When you absolutely have to hit the ball straight, try teeing the ball a little lower. It won't curve as much to the left or right.

MY SHOULDERS AND ARMS MATCH UP

One swing problem I have to monitor constantly is not letting my arms lag too far behind my upper body on the downswing. Because my hips and shoulders unwind so quickly, they sometimes outrace my arms. The result is that I drag the clubhead into the ball from far inside the target line, forcing me to rotate my hands furiously to square the clubface at impact. If I don't rotate the hands enough I push the ball to the right; if I rotate them too much I hit a big hook. This makes for an inconsistent ball flight.

My goal, as you can see in this photo taken just after impact, is to keep my arms in front of my body as much as possible throughout the downswing. Notice that my arms are in front of my chest, my shoulders aligned only slightly left of the target line. I've timed everything very well on this swing, and you can bet the ball flew a mile in a controlled direction.

■ My head remains well to my right, my arms swinging past my body.

■ My right elbow is directly in front of my right hip. That's a sign of good control.

■ At impact my clubshaft is vertical, just as it was at address.

■ Centrifugal force straightens and extends my left arm.

■ The label on my golf glove is visible, proof I haven't rotated my hands excessively.

■ A good 80 percent of my weight is on my left leg and foot.

AT THE FINISH, MY RIGHT FOOT COMES UP, EXPOSING ALL OF MY SPIKES.

FANCY FOOTWORK

. . . .

A lot has been said and written about footwork during the swing, but I've never looked at the feet as super-active components. I believe the feet merely react to the motion occurring elsewhere in your body. If your footwork appears loose and sloppy, it's because something else in your swing isn't right.

I allow my right foot to come off the ground just before impact. I really have no choice; my hips and shoulders rotate so fast and my weight has shifted so aggressively, I'd hurt my back if I kept my right heel on the ground. If my right heel stays glued to the turf, I'm not using my lower body enough.

A Sign of Good Balance

At the finish, I've "released" my right foot, allowing it to come up on its toe. That's evidence of proper weight distribution throughout the downswing and a full, complete follow-through. At the finish, I should be able to hold this position without losing my balance.

MY SWING THROUGH THE AGES

· · · · · · · · · ·

I was a decent player at age 16, good enough to have won two U.S. Junior Amateur titles with a third on the way. But my full-swing technique then was not as sound as it would be at age 20, and nowhere near as good as at age 24. There is always room for improvement, and a careful look at these sequence photos shows just how far I've come.

The biggest area of improvement is apparent in the way I use my lower body. As a kid, I really whipped my hips and shoulders through the ball on the downswing. They moved so fast my arms simply couldn't keep up. It put huge demands on my timing. I've since learned to make my hips, shoulders and arms work more in sync. My goal of becoming a more consistent, versatile ball striker is finally within reach.

AGE 16

AGE 20

AGE 24

Please turn the page →

I SHAKE HANDS WITH THE TARGET

One of Butch Harmon's favorite reminders on the follow-through is to "shake hands with the target." My right arm is fully extended straight down the target line. That shows I've tried to generate as much clubhead speed as possible.

I can tell that I hit a draw on this shot just by looking at the photo, because my right forearm is rolling over the left. That's a sign of natural hand rotation—of moving the clubface to a square or slightly closed position.

HOW I HIT MY DRIVER OFF THE DECK

．．．．．．．．．．．．．．．．．．．．．．．．．．．

When playing super-long par-5 holes, I occasionally have so far to go on my second shot that my 3-wood just won't get me there. If my lie is very good, I'll hit my driver from the fairway. It's a tough shot to pull off consistently, but the reward can be great—in some cases I can get 300 yards out of the shot.

The first thing I do is play the ball about an inch farther back in my stance than normal. I also position my hands so they are almost even with the ball. I open my stance a bit as well; that's because I play a fade exclusively on this shot.

I make a very long backswing, making sure I turn my shoulders as fully as possible. This shot is all about good timing, so I make sure I don't

rush. I start down slowly and then let my swing gather speed, so the clubhead is just ripping through the air by the time it gets to the ball. I want to sweep the ball cleanly off the turf without taking any divot at all. When everything happens just right, the ball takes off like a bullet to the left of the target, makes a little turn to the right, then runs a good distance after it lands.

MY SETUP AND SWING ARE DESIGNED TO SWEEP THE BALL OFF THE TURF.

FOILING A VERY FAST CAMERA

· · · · · · · · · · · · · · · · · · · ·

To this point I've talked very little about how much clubhead speed I actually generate through impact. Here are the numbers from an analysis made in 1998: Through the hitting area my clubhead is moving at 119 m.p.h., with my ball coming off the clubface at 180 m.p.h. That isn't as fast as some of the guys who enter national long-drive contests, but it's definitely up there for a PGA Tour pro. The result is plenty of distance with every club in the bag. The game became much easier for me when I was capable of reaching most par-5 holes in two shots and was able to

hit the ball higher and softer with less effort.

The photos you see here and on the following pages were shot in 1998. The camera we use for these types of swing sequences is known as the Hulcher. It can shoot up to 65 frames per second. It doesn't sound like a camera; it makes a whirring, rat-a-tat sound as the spool of film advances. The frames appear in reverse order, reading from right to left, due to the way the film is loaded.

When the photographs taken that day were developed, the editors of *Golf Digest* informed me of a unique problem: They didn't have many shots of me precisely at impact. My clubhead moved through the ball so quickly that the camera only caught the moment of truth a few times. The next time they photographed my swing, they asked me to make a few extra swings from each angle, to be sure they caught my club in contact with the ball.

I GIVE MY BACKSWING A
HEAD START BY TILTING MY
UPPER BODY SLIGHTLY TO
MY RIGHT AT ADDRESS.

FULL EXTENSION EARLY
CREATES A WIDE,
POWERFUL SWING ARC.

MY ARMS ARE DIRECTLY
IN FRONT OF MY CHEST,
THE SIGNATURE OF A
WELL-TIMED DOWNSWING.

ALTHOUGH I'VE SHIFTED
MY WEIGHT TO MY LEFT,
MY HEAD IS FARTHER
TO MY RIGHT THAN IT
WAS AT ADDRESS.

THIS IS THE ONLY MOMENT
IN THE SWING WHEN BOTH
MY ARMS ARE EXTENDED
TO THE MAX.

I KNOW I'VE MADE A
GOOD SWING WHEN I FEEL
BALANCED AT THE FINISH.

MY STANCE IS WIDE
ENOUGH TO PROVIDE
STABILITY, NARROW
ENOUGH TO TURN FREELY.

I NEVER LET MY WEIGHT
STRAY TO THE OUTSIDE
OF MY RIGHT FOOT.

THE CLUB DOESN'T HAVE
TO REACH PARALLEL FOR
ME TO GENERATE POWER.

I LET THE CLUB "FALL"
INTO POSITION EARLY
IN THE DOWNSWING.

WITH MY RIGHT ARM CLOSE
TO MY SIDE, I'M LIKE A
BOXER READY TO DELIVER
AN UPPERCUT.

I'M UNWINDING MY HIPS
AS FAST AS THEY CAN
POSSIBLY GO.

MY HEAD IS STILL DOWN, A
SIGN I'VE "STAYED WITH THE
SHOT" INSTEAD OF BAILING
OUT WITH MY UPPER BODY.

THIS IS WHY I HAVE TO TUCK MY SHIRT IN A FEW TIMES A ROUND.

DRIVER EDUCATION

Let me follow through by reviewing the key points I've made in this chapter:

■ The width of my stance should be wide enough to provide stability, but narrow enough to promote a full body turn.

■ I hold my head high at address so my left shoulder can turn under my chin.

■ On the backswing, I make sure my hips turn but don't slide.

■ I make my backswing as wide as possible by extending my hands away from my right hip and turning my shoulders as far as they'll go.

■ I turn my shoulders fully, but don't allow the club to dip past parallel.

■ For good timing, I keep my hands and arms in front of my chest throughout the swing.

■ For power with no loss of accuracy, I extend my right hand straight down the target line after impact.

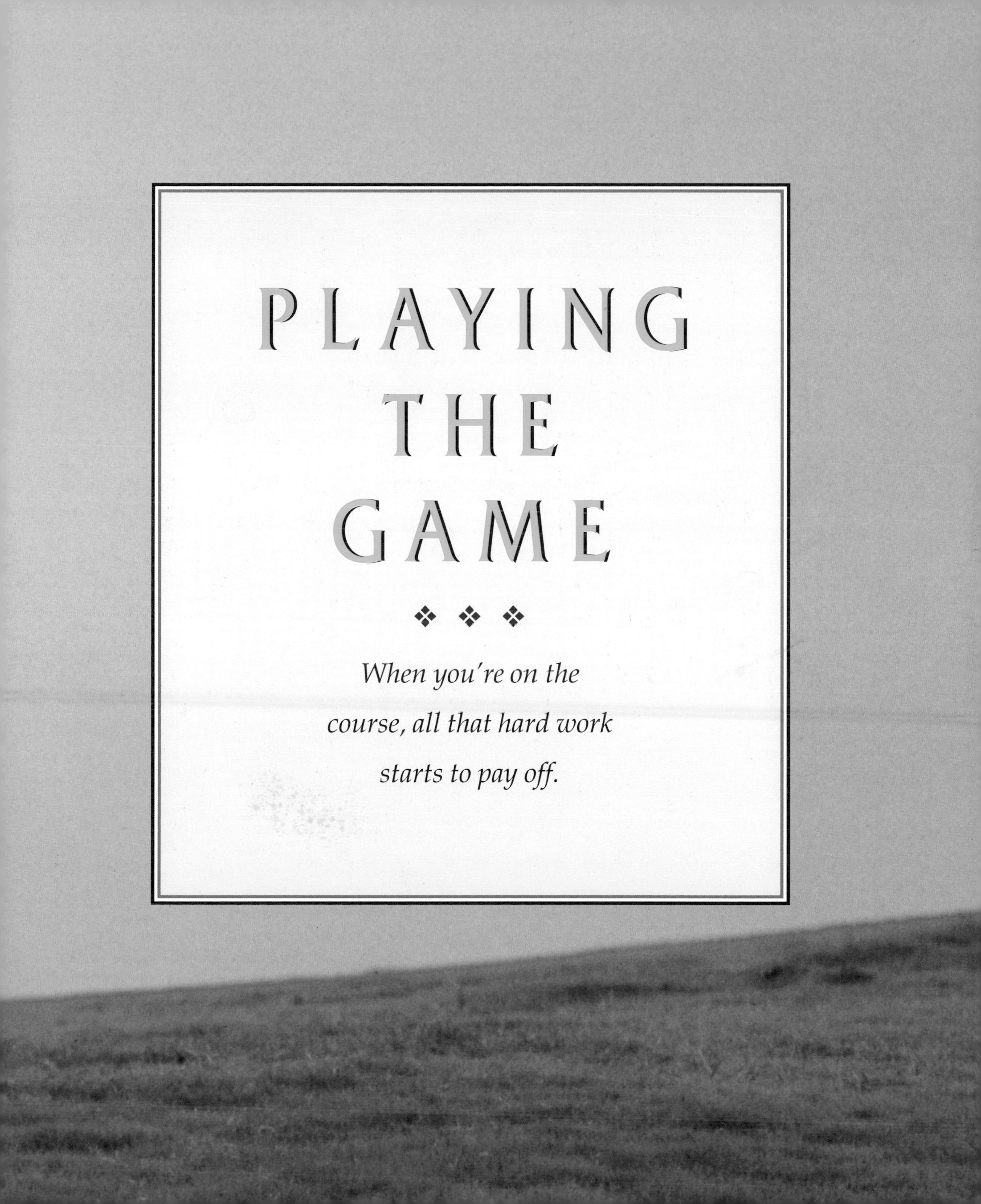

PLAYING THE GAME

❖ ❖ ❖

When you're on the

course, all that hard work

starts to pay off.

*❖*8*❖*
HOW TO HANDLE
PROBLEMS

WHEN IT STARTS GETTING UGLY

If you play this game long enough, eventually you'll face some adversity. It's how you handle those days when the game gets mean and shows its ugly side that defines who you are as a competitor. I've had my share of those days, perhaps none more memorable, or forgettable, than the first Thursday in April of 1997. It is the case of the missing golf swing. Not quite worthy of Agatha Christie but a mystery nonetheless.

It's funny. I didn't feel that nervous when I stepped on the first tee at Augusta National during the first round of the Masters. I mean no more nervous than usual. I certainly didn't feel too bad. I felt pretty good about my game that week and pretty good about my putting, too. Then, all of a sudden, I hit a pull hook off the tee. The ball ducked into the rough like a jackrabbit and nestled into a bed of pine needles among the trees. Just like that I made bogey. Not the kind of start I'd planned. To make matters worse, I failed to make birdie at No. 2, a par 5 reachable for average-length tour players. Things progressively went downhill from there.

I hit one of the worst shots ever at the par-3 fourth. The pin was in the back-left corner. The wind was kind of swirling in that corner of the golf course, going back and forth from straight right-to-left to into me from the left. But when I finished my preshot routine and set up to hit the ball, I knew exactly which way it was blowing. So I went ahead and hit it. The ball flared about 30 yards short and 40 yards off line, finishing in the bamboo trees on the right. I didn't even know there were bamboo trees over there. I actually did well to make bogey, but the roller-coaster continued its descent.

When I got to the 10th tee I was four over par and kind of in a state of shock, like a fighter who has taken a good shot to the chin. I glanced at the giant scoreboard over at 18 and saw that four-under was leading. I was only eight back. I had a little talk with myself. "You know what? If I can get to even par I'll be right in this ballgame." Because

Some of my most frustrating moments have come from plugged lies, like this one at Royal Troon's No. 8.

far right and instead of riding the wind as much as I thought, the ball dived into the bunker and plugged. Took me two to get out of that beach sand and I three-putted for triple. Any chance I had of winning disappeared right there.

But my most embarrassing train wreck occurred at Jack Nicklaus' tournament—the Memorial—in 1997. I remember a thunderstorm rolling in and it raining buckets. It took five days to finish the event. At the third hole, a short par 4 that normally requires a lay up with an iron off the tee to avoid the water hazard, I spun my approach from 115 yards into the water. After repeating the same shot, I finally got one on the green, which by now was soaking wet. The horn had sounded suspending play, but I was determined to finish the

I'm exasperated watching the ball roll back at my feet before I finally get it out on the second try.

hole. I hit my first putt about halfway to the hole, then two-putted from there for 9. Besides hitting two of the worst shots I'd hit in a long time, I compounded the problem by totally losing my concentration. So, not only can swing faults lead to trouble, frustration can double it, or in this case, quintuple it.

Even if you fix swing faults, which I was finally able to do by the 1999 season, you're still not going to make a perfect swing every time. A big reason for my success is the fact that my misses are not as bad as they once were. I have fewer train wrecks. Sometimes, even when you're swinging well, bad breaks can throw you off. Knowing how to play trouble shots can help with damage control and keep you from making a bad situation worse.

KNOW WHEN—AND WHEN NOT—TO BE A HERO

· ·

When I do hit an errant tee shot, I've learned to accept it and just get the ball back into play—most of the time. There are times, though—if I'm 2 down with two to play and have to make birdie, for example—that I will still try to hit the heroic shot. That's also part of what makes the game fun. I relish successful escapes, but believe me, I assess the percentages before I attempt one. At the 1999 Phoenix Open, I had a little help from my friends, and I didn't need to be a hero.

THE LOW HOOK—I CURVE THE BALL WITH MY BIG MUSCLES

I've had plenty of practice on this particular shot, especially when I was younger and had less control of my driver. First you must set up with a slightly wider stance than normal and position the ball slightly back of center. Aim your feet, hips and shoulders squarely, but to the right of the target. Take the club back low and wide along the line of your feet. Regulate the amount of hook by how much you toe-in the club at address, not by manipulating the clubhead with the hands during the swing. A general rule of thumb: I aim my body lines (feet, hips, shoulders) at a point where I want the ball to start, and I aim the clubface where I want the ball to finish. That simplifies the manipulation of the clubface.

I work the ball with my big muscles. Most amateurs aim too far to the right, get very steep on the backswing and too vertical on the down-swing. The result is often a fat shot. Instead, feel as if you're making a sweeping motion with the club, and swing through the ball from inside the target line.

I PLAY THE BALL BACK IN MY STANCE AND TOE-IN THE CLUBFACE.

THE BIG CUT—I KEEP CLUB'S TOE FROM TURNING LEFT

I like to visualize the ball flight—where I want the ball to start and finish—then commit to it. I use one to two more clubs than normal for the distance the shot has to cover. I open my stance and the clubface slightly at address and play the ball back or forward in my stance, depending upon how low or high I need to hit it. The swing path should be a little more outside on the backswing and inside after impact. Limit the release of the club through the shot, keeping the toe of the club from turning to the left.

When you really need
to curve the ball—
exaggerate everything.

THWAK!

I DON'T LET A SAND DIVOT FREAK ME OUT

We all have had shots somehow find their way to some strange destinations. I've seen mine wind up in the middle of a gorse thicket, in front of a fist-sized rock, up against a tree stump and directly behind

a giant boulder, just to name a few. Most of those were the result of an errant tee shot. What leaves me scratching my head is when I hit a perfect drive and the ball lands in a sand divot. When that happens, it helps to have a positive outlook in a negative situation. Believing you can execute a shot is as important as knowing how to do it.

Play It Back and Pick It
A sand divot hole is just a miniature fairway bunker, and the shot should be executed like a fairway bunker shot. Play the ball back in your stance slightly more than normal. That will help you contact the ball first—critical to playing the shot. Stand a little taller at address so you can pick the ball off the sand, just as you would in a fairway bunker. Your backswing should be a little steeper than normal, which will also help you contact the ball first, then the sand. Select one more club than you normally need for the yardage, so you can swing easier and keep your balance. Average players often try to beat down on the ball or scoop it from a sand divot. Instead, think of extending the divot as you swing through the ball. That will ensure solid contact.

One of my key thoughts: Just like in a fairway bunker, I try to keep my lower body quiet on this shot, swinging mostly my arms. That will also help ensure a solid hit, which is crucial from this type of lie.

I KEEP MY LOWER BODY STILL AND EXTEND THE DIVOT.

MUDDER THAN HECK

. . . .

I've played the game long enough never to question the fairness of it. Sometimes, though, I'm tempted—like when, because of course conditions or an unlucky bounce, my ball picks up mud. The key to playing a mudball is understanding how mud affects ball flight. As a rule of thumb, the ball will go in the opposite direction of the mud. If mud is on the left side of the ball the tendency is for the ball to travel more to the right than normal and vice versa. What makes the shot more problematic is determining the direction and distance it will travel. Also, the harder you swing, the more spin you impart on the ball, causing it to move more off line.

I Adjust My Setup and Swing Speed

Because mud on the right side of the ball means it will go left, I must adjust my setup to allow for that movement. The last thing I want to do is accentuate ball movement. So, to control ball flight, I select one more club than normal and make a softer swing. Finally, I must have ample extension on the follow-through to a less-than-full finish, an indication that I didn't quit on the shot.

I DON'T GET WATERLOGGED

My adventures with water hazards have been mostly the deep-six standard, making a drop the only choice. But on occasion I have been confronted with a partially submerged ball. It's not the most difficult shot when proper technique is applied. My first move is to take off my shoes and socks and put on my rain suit. Then I approach the shot exactly like I would a greenside bunker explosion. I open my stance and clubface. Then I position the ball toward the front of my stance and focus on a spot about an inch behind the ball. I cock my wrists quickly on the backswing to a full wristcock and take the club up steeply just as I would on a normal bunker shot. I swing about 50 percent harder, though, because of the water's density compared with sand. My final thought is to accelerate through impact. I don't want to quit on the shot. I'm always more than a little nervous about being an unwanted guest in some creature's habitat, so rather than rush the shot, I prefer to let my caddie test the water first.

I KEEP MY COOL IN THE HEAT

· · · · · · · · · · · · · · · · · · · ·

Sometimes playing conditions contribute to golf's ugliness. As a native southern Californian, I'm a warm-weather player. I like it when the greens are rolling fast and the mercury is rising. Of course, sometimes it gets so hot it can affect your game physically and mentally.

I love returning to my mom's homeland, but it seems every time I go to Thailand for a tournament they're in the middle of a heat wave. On my trip there for the 2000 Johnnie Walker Classic, it was about 100 degrees every day with humidity to match. Thanks to physical conditioning I'm able to endure the heat, but I also take several precautions when it gets too hot. I also use common sense to help me handle extremely cold and rainy conditions.

■ I wear light colors as much as possible, except the final round when I must wear red.

■ I avoid becoming dehydrated by drinking plenty of water.

■ I like to eat fruit (apples and bananas) and/or fruit bars to keep my potassium level up. I also like energy bars because they seem to be easier to digest.

■ I dampen one end of my towel and use it as a cooling agent. I keep the other end dry for the moisture on my hands and grips.

■ I wear a cap to keep the direct sunshine from my head.

■ I have at least a half-dozen gloves available so I can change as often as necessary.

■ I walk slower between shots to conserve energy.

■ I focus only on what I can control—my next shot—not things I can't, like the heat.

HOW I KEEP MY
ENGINE FROM FREEZING

nlike most other sports, golf is sometimes played in the foulest weather. When it's cold outside, I want to be sure to stay warm inside. Here's how I do it.

■ Silk undergarments help keep in my body heat.

■ I prefer a layering of lightweight clothing instead of a heavy parka.

■ Since most of my body heat escapes through my head, I wear a dark hat, often a wool ski cap.

■ I'm not one for wool mittens—they just don't look manly—but I will use one of those glycerin heat packs to keep my hands warm.

■ I might do some extra stretching because cold weather tends to restrict muscles.

■ I walk faster between shots to produce more body heat.

■ I focus only on what I can control, and I can't control the weather.

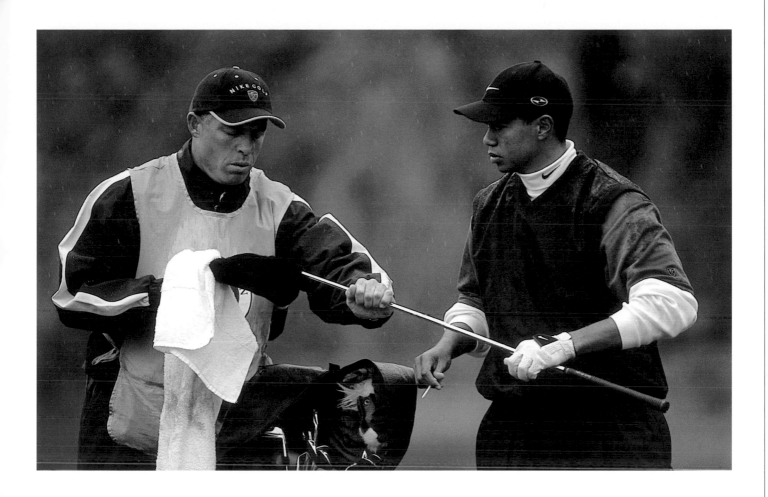

HOW I KEEP FROM FEELING ALL WET

Whoever said it never rains on the golf course never played tournament golf. Even in casual play, rain can ruin a perfectly good time if I'm not prepared. Here are my waterproofing tips:

■ I use a sturdy, windproof umbrella.

■ I keep a good quantity of gloves in my bag and change as necessary.

■ I keep an extra towel in my umbrella.

■ I have learned that a good rain suit is a must.

■ I keep an extra pair of socks available.

■ I wear a cap to keep my head dry.

■ I sometimes turn the bill of my cap backward so water doesn't drip through my vision as I bend over to chip or putt.

■ I try to play to my normal pace and rhythm. I don't let inclement weather make me rush a shot.

■ I focus only on what I can control—my game—despite the conditions.

KNOCK IT
DOWN, NOT OUT

· ·

From the start my intention was to be an international player, so I developed a love for links courses. Of course, that meant I had to become a decent wind player if I wanted to be successful internationally. My coach Butch Harmon taught me a shot during the 1995 U.S. Amateur at Newport (R.I.) Country Club that I've employed many times since to combat windy conditions. The knockdown is one of those shots that, when executed properly, can anchor your game even in gale-force winds.

Take More Club and Swing Easy

The knockdown allows you to control ball trajectory. The less air time the ball has, the less it will be affected by the wind. The key to controlling distance against a strong wind is to take more club and swing easy. That reduces backspin. The average player tries to hit the ball too hard against the wind. That just adds backspin and makes the ball balloon up in the air.

Sit On It

Take a stance that's a little wider than normal, and at address try to "sit down" by bending your knees slightly more than normal. Position the ball slightly back of center in your stance. Take a three-quarter backswing, keeping the club very low and wide on the takeaway.

Think Low and Wide

You want to swing relatively wide both back and down. A common amateur mistake is to make a steep downswing and take a deep divot. The ball shoots up in the air because of increased backspin. Through impact, keep your hands low and your finish abbreviated and balanced. The result should be a shot that flies low and is minimally affected by the wind.

I keep my hands low, my finish short. For more specifics on how I hit the knockdown, see "How I Whip the Wind" on the following pages.

HOW I WHIP THE WIND

When the wind is howling, I want the ball to spend as little time in the air as possible. That means hitting the knock-down—the low, wind-cheating shot that can keep my score intact in even the most vicious winds.

I Program My Ball Flight

I make three preswing adjustments. First, I position the ball back in my stance, just to the right of center. Next I choose more club, both to reduce loft and allow me to make an easier swing. Finally, I widen my stance for extra stability and flex my knees more than usual. I'm all set to drill the ball through any breeze.

I Shorten Swing, Keep Hands Low

The knockdown shot is all about control. Balance is a must. So, I make only a three-quarter backswing, trusting my less-lofted club selection to achieve the distance I need.

I keep my swing fairly wide both back and down. I swing through the ball on a shallow angle, taking a very thin divot. I don't hit down on the ball too steeply, as that causes the ball to balloon up into the wind. I also keep my hands very low into the follow-through, swinging through to a fairly short finish. Follow these rules, and you'll be amazed at how little effect the wind has on your shots.

I PLAY THE BALL BACK IN MY STANCE AND FINISH LOW TO HIT THE BALL LOW.

I DON'T SWING BACK FARTHER THAN THIS.

I TRY TO KEEP MY HANDS BELOW MY BELT.

SQUARE FLIES STRAIGHT.

TWO DEADLY BALL FLIGHTS

If you're spending too much time in trouble, there's a good chance that what is making golf so ugly is your swing. It is probably totally out of control. Most of my high-handicap pro-am partners suffer from either of two deadly ball flights— the right-to-right push slice or the left-to-left pull hook.

If You Slice the Ball

The clubface is open at impact. Often the culprit is the wrists and/or the forearms. The forearms rotate too much on the takeaway and the left wrist is cupped at the top of the backswing. The result is an open clubface at the top, meaning it points more vertically than horizontally. Open at the top usually means open at the bottom, too, and a huge slice. Combine that with a swing path too much from the inside and the ball has to go right. You want more of a flat left wrist and a square clubface at the top of the backswing. You can attain that position by having quieter hands and restricting forearm rotation on the backswing. Use a mirror to check the angle created by your left wrist. The more cupped it is, the more likely you'll hit a banana ball.

If You Hook the Ball

The clubface is closed at impact. Most hookers suffer from a lack of body rotation on the through swing. They start with the chin buried in the chest on the takeaway and never really rotate fully away from the ball on the backswing. Since they can't unwind what they don't wind up in the first place, they fail to rotate fully toward the target. What small amount of weight they have transferred to the right side remains there. To compensate on the downswing, they flip their wrists, toeing in the club and producing a snapper—the ball starts left and then hooks. To fix the problem, stay connected. That is, make sure the triangle created by your hands, arms and chest at address remains intact throughout the swing. If you maintain that connection, your weight will naturally shift into your right side on the backswing and transfer to your left side on the downswing.

CUPPED CAUSES SLICE.

BOWED CAUSES HOOK.

SOMETIMES UGLY IS NOT SO BAD

· · · · · · · · · · · · · · · ·

On the final playoff hole of the 2000 PGA Championship at Valhalla Country Club in Louisville, I nearly pull-hooked my tee shot into the parking lot. Fortunately, it bounced off a tree and onto a cartpath, rolling into a playable lie and averting what could have been a disaster. I managed to get the ball back into play, then hit my approach on the par 5 into a greenside bunker. From there I exploded to within two feet of the hole. A very ugly par secured my fifth professional major.

*A key to my success:
I develop a game plan
and try to stick to it.*

❖9❖
HOW TO STAY IN CONTROL

MANAGING YOUR GAME

Pop had a mantra. "Son," he would say, "you get out of it what you put into it." When I would get frustrated, those words were gentle persuasion to try again. Because of them I understood very early that no matter how many physical gifts a person might have, to refine them, you must bust your butt. I quickly bought into the idea that the road to success is paved with sweat and calluses. I also was taught how to manage the game instead of letting the game manage me. Pop has often told the story about my first lesson in course management. I don't remember it. Heck, I was barely out of training pants at the time. But I believe in its veracity because my course management today is a reflection of it.

As the story goes, Pop and I were playing the Navy course near my home in Cypress, Calif. On the second hole, I hit my drive behind a large clump of trees. Pop asked me what I was going to do. I looked at him as if to say, "What do you mean?" He said, "Son, I'm going to make two contributions to your golf game. One is mental toughness and the other course management. Now what are you going to do, Tiger?" I said, "I can hit the ball underneath the trees, but there's a great big sand trap in front of the green." Pop nodded. I said, "I can't hit the ball over the trees because they're too tall." Pop nodded again. I said, "I can hit my ball back into the fairway, then onto the green and one-putt for par." He said, "Son, that is course management."

Pop was ex-military and definitely "old school." He believes there is a standard operating procedure (SOP) for every undertaking, including golf. But when he sprang that one on me, I did what any 3-year-old would do—I asked why. He explained to me that the starting point of every shot is behind the ball. That you must visualize the shot and access all of the potential problems, then commit to the shot that you want to hit. I didn't realize it at the time, but my most important lesson in course management began with Pop's insistence that I have a preshot routine. Every so often I would forget to go through my routine but before long it became ingrained. In fact, I believe it helped me win my very first Southern California Junior Golf Association tournament.

I must have looked pretty regimented as I went through my routine, but I didn't care. It's what I knew, and I felt comfortable. Not many of the other kids approached the game that way. Well, I shot 120 but I won. Mom and Pop were so proud of me. I guess I was pretty proud, too. By the way, I use that same preshot routine today. It doesn't matter what your individual preshot routine is, just as long as you do it the same way every time and you don't hold up play.

Great players operate "in the moment." In other words, they never get ahead of themselves. And they never, ever appear overwhelmed by any situation. One of the reasons I'm able to hit good shots is because I go through the same routine. I learned it from my dad, who had read it from Jack Nicklaus. It's been said that you can put a stopwatch on Nicklaus and his routine will be the same every time. Granted, his might be a little slower than most guys, but it is his natural rhythm. If you notice, my preshot routine doesn't vary and it is uniquely mine. It helps me remain calm and in the present, prepared to execute a shot to the best of my ability.

The starting point of every shot is behind the ball. I home in on the target by shrinking my field of vision...

From there I simply move into the shot and make a couple of waggles...

Preparation is a big part of course management. It's like cramming for a final exam. You want to be armed with all the answers so you can score your best. The first thing I do to prepare for a tournament is clear my mind. I don't dwell on what I did or didn't do in the event just completed. I might reflect on it later but I won't clutter my head with things I have no control over. I want to start every tournament fresh mentally. Freeing my mind of everything that has happened up to that point is how I accomplish it.

When I was an amateur, my dad and I would come up with a game plan for how to play certain holes. As a matter of fact, the first time I played the Masters (in 1995) I spent many hours reviewing videotapes of telecasts to get a feel for Augusta National. Then I put a game plan together. Of course, you don't want to be too rigid in your approach. I eventually grew out of that routine because I felt it wasn't flexible enough. Now I prefer to go in with a blank slate and let the situation dictate what I can or cannot do. True, I'm equipped with a much better swing now so I can more easily handle different situations. That also keeps me from forming preconceived notions of what club I have to hit off a certain tee, because situations change. Sometimes you need to be more aggressive; other times less aggressive. You have to be flexible.

I look at the target one last time…

Then I pull the trigger.

When I'm preparing for a familiar course like Augusta National and have a week off to get ready, I like to go home and practice. I specifically work on certain shots I'll need during the tournament. For example, I know that I need to hit a sweeping draw tee shot on the par-5 13th because of the pine seedlings that were planted in the right rough. I will work on that shot extensively to give myself a better chance of executing it under the gun. If a course is set up similar to a major championship like Muirfield Village was in 2000 two weeks prior to the U.S. Open at Pebble Beach, I'll practice shots that I might need in the major. That year the greenside rough at Muirfield Village was about four inches in some spots and the greens were firm and typically fast, just like I knew they would be at Pebble. So I practiced hitting that little "chop" shot from the rough, letting the ball feed to the hole. It not only came in handy for me in the Memorial, which I won, but it was a big part of my arsenal during the Open victory.

Practice rounds are crucial when I'm playing a course for the first time. That's when my caddie and I get to know the lay of the land. We have a laundry list of things we look for, from what shape of shot to hit on each hole to how receptive the greens are to shots of varying trajectories. The successful golfer not only knows what he can do but what he can't afford to do.

Another factor you must take into account when preparing for a tournament is type of course—links or parkland, short and tight or long and wide open. I've grown to prefer links courses like those in the British Open rota, because they are the ultimate challenge to a player's creativity and resourcefulness. We play mostly parkland courses on the PGA Tour and are faced with the same kind of target golf week in and week out that turns most tournaments into putting

Get in the habit of preparing yourself for upcoming tournaments and rounds. Part of my preparation for the challenges of Augusta National includes watching videos of past Masters. Knowing how the course plays in various conditions factors into my overall game plan.

I factor in all the information available to me before selecting a club and executing the shot.

contests. Both types of courses might place the same demands on your ball striking but require different shots. For example, you can get away with the occasional errant tee shot on a parkland course, where long-ball hitters with high trajectories thrive. Hit that same drive on a true links course and you might wind up waist deep in "love" grass or even worse, a gorse thicket. You can also hit a wider variety of shots on links courses, including knockdowns, bump-and-runs and high, soft shots. Factor in the wind—where one minute you're hitting a 9-iron 180 yards and the next a 3-iron 150—and you

can appreciate the need for knowing how to play different kinds of shots, plus having the nerve to play them when the situation dictates.

I'm not a happy camper when a course is deliberately set up to take the driver out of the hands of long hitters like myself. I don't mind six-inch rough as long as it's not brought into play by altering the course. I've had to adapt to shrinking landing areas, sometimes as little as 30 yards wide. Adaptability is another part of course management. Sometimes you just have to take what the game—and/or course superintendent—gives you.

THE DO'S AND DON'TS OF COURSE MANAGEMENT

- **DO** establish a game plan before the round—not during it.

- **DO** get the correct yardage to both the front of the green and to the flagstick.

- **DO** know when to go for it and when to play safe.

- **DO** accept that there is such a thing as a "good" bogey.

- **DO** shape your shots off the tee to take one side of the fairway out of play.

- **DO** play your own game; let your opponent play his.

- **DON'T** let an inflated ego do the same thing to your score. Avoid the "big" number.

- **DON'T** chuck it at the first sign of trouble. Stick with it.

- **DON'T** get fooled by sucker pins; play to the fat of the green when necessary.

- **DON'T** attempt a specialty shot in competition that you haven't practiced.

- **DON'T** ever aim your shot so that if it goes straight it will wind up in trouble.

- **DON'T** forget that it's just a game. Have fun.

I always try to be prepared for the unexpected, like those times when I have to rely on my creativity and imagination to pull me out of a tight spot. That's one of the reasons I love links golf so much. You get to use every ounce of your creativity, sometimes on the same hole. For example, 200-yard 9-irons and 100-foot putts are not uncommon. Being able to control distance and trajectory is critical at any venue, especially those with island greens.

Never aim a tee shot toward trouble, hoping your natural fade or draw will bring it back into play. You never want to be penalized for a straight shot.

DON'T AIM THIS WAY

KNOW WHEN TO HOLD 'EM AND WHEN TO FOLD 'EM

The most common mistake amateurs make is grabbing the driver on a hole that was designed to be played as a lay up. Sometimes conditions (for example, if the hole is playing downwind) and circumstances (if your opponent is dormie) require that you pull out the driver and go for it. Make sure the reward is worth the risk. Most often, though, it's best to play the percentages. Use a long iron or a utility wood and play to a certain yardage. By that I mean, if you know the water hazard is 225 yards from the tee, use a club that when struck solidly will hit the ball short of the hazard. Also, if you have a "pet" distance for your approach, say 110 yards, hit the club that will leave you that yardage into the green. Manage the course; don't let it manage you.

I have been known to buck the odds, usually when I felt I had nothing to lose and everything to gain. I fought my way back into contention in the final round of the 1997 AT&T Pebble Beach National Pro-Am and was just a couple shots back of my friend Mark O'Meara when I got to 18. Even though I killed my drive, I still had more than 270 yards to the green and the wind was not that favorable. I really never thought of laying up. I felt I needed to eagle the hole to force a possible playoff, so I had to go for it. Fortunately, my driver off the deck found the green. Although I missed the putt and finished a shot behind Marko, I felt good that I didn't back off a green-light opportunity. Had it been another situation, say if I was tied for the lead or up by one, I wouldn't have risked hitting my second shot into the ocean.

Managing my game means knowing when to forgo the driver off the tee. Often, the closer to the green you hit the ball on a short par 4, the more bunkers and water come into play. My standard control club is the 2-iron. For some players, it may be a 4- or 5-wood. The higher loft creates more backspin, and less sidespin, for more control. Plus, a shorter club means a wayward shot will not go as far off line.

Course management includes knowing when to go for it and when to lay up. I will often hit a 3-wood or a long iron off the tee when I know the risk is not worth the reward.

FIND YOUR NATURAL RHYTHM

When I'm really on, course management becomes almost second nature. It seems that I know instinctively what shot to play. If most of the trouble is behind the greens, then you can believe my misses aren't going to be long. If there is trouble to the left, I make sure my shot is shaped to avoid that trouble. And I don't really have to think about it. I call it finding your natural rhythm. Every golfer has one, and it starts during your preround warm-up.

I also adopted my preround practice routine from Jack Nicklaus. I always use the same six clubs, working my way up from the sand wedge to the driver. The last club I hit is the one I intend to use on my first shot of the day. My purpose is not to work on my swing. If I don't have it when I arrive at the course, I'm not going to find it in a 30-minute warm-up. My purpose is to establish my rhythm. I want to make sure I go out there with the right rhythm. That's when I'm on. When I'm out of rhythm I can't find the on switch and every swing becomes problematic. How I manage my game that particular day can mean the difference between hanging in there or shooting myself out of it. Fortunately, I've been able to hang in more times than not. And so can you.

KEYS TO CONTROL

While the game itself at times appears to move in slow motion, some things occur in a millisecond that can have a dramatic effect on the execution of a shot or outcome of a tournament. Knowing how and when to jack yourself up and calm yourself down are two of those things. For example, if I need to hit a big drive and I've been a little lethargic, I can get the adrenaline going immediately. On the other hand, I can throttle back on a shot simply by composing myself and inducing calm. No one can do it for you. You have to do it yourself. It's a matter of being in touch with yourself mentally, physically and emotionally.

At times I've had to fight off negative energy as well as a loose golf swing.

❖ 10 ❖
HOW TO MASTER
THE MIND

WINNING PSYCHOLOGY

The true essence of golf is capitalizing on opportunities and minimizing mistakes. It is a thinking man's (or woman's) game to a great degree. I believe that my creative mind is my greatest weapon. The best way to describe it is a kind of inner vision that enables me to see things others might not, like a certain way to play a shot or a slight opening in a thicket. And I've been blessed with the physical ability to execute whatever shot my mind dictates. Your creative mind should be your greatest weapon, too. While managing your game, you should be constantly assessing situations, factoring in variables like changing course conditions and deciding on whether or not to play the percentages. The psychology of golf goes a step further than course management. It entails mental toughness, self-confidence, intimidation, gamesmanship, conquering inner demons, instant recall of past successes and being able to quickly purge failures. It is the game within the game.

Mental toughness was the second gift to my game from my dad. He wanted to make sure that my powers of concentration could withstand any and all distractions. Golf is not a game for fragile psyches so he worked to strengthen mine. He established two rules from the outset. First, he forbade me to talk during a round in which he pulled every dirty trick in the book, from dropping a set of clubs in the middle of my backswing to walking directly in my line of sight as I stroked a putt. The second rule was that there were no more rules. Anything goes. And it did. He had no idea whether I could hold up under such difficult circumstances, so he provided me with an out—a secret code word that only the two of us knew. Don't ask me how or why—perhaps it was pure stubbornness—but I never used it. The toughest part was not talking, although if looks could kill, my pop would not have made it through my formative years. Pop delivered on his promise.

Some distractions are easier to block out than others. For example, I've learned to deal with camera shutters going off in the middle of my swing. I still get upset when it

I was taught that it's healthy to let it all go after an emotionally draining event.

happens, but my reaction is directed at the offender more than the offense. I realize that fame comes with a price. I don't know how I can stop in the middle of my downswing. I just know when it's necessary. In retrospect, I guess that's what Pop was preparing me for. Other distractions, however, can knock the wind out of you like a blow to the solar plexus. The key is not letting them affect your performance. That's what happened to me during the final round of the 1999 PGA Championship at Medinah. I had survived some loose swings and managed to go up by five shots with eight holes to play. Two holes later, I'm standing on the tee box of the par-3 13th when Sergio Garcia holes a birdie putt to cut my lead to three. I'm sure he felt the game was on but I was concentrating on what I had to do, realizing that was the only thing I could control. I made an unlucky double bogey on 13 when my tee shot wound up in the deep rough just off the green about 20 feet

from the hole. As I walked to the 14th tee I felt something I never had in competition. All of a sudden the crowd, which had been so gracious and supportive all week, seemed to switch its allegiance to Sergio. Perhaps they were naturally rooting for the underdog or wanted a close finish. I don't know, but I could feel the negative energy directed toward me. When I holed the little 18-incher for a one-shot win, I let out a huge sigh of relief. I not only withstood the challenge of a gritty, young challenger and a truly tough stretch of finishing holes in a major championship, I did it against some difficult psychological warfare. I was mentally and emotionally drained.

Confidence is easier to define than it is to measure. It is an assuredness in one's ability to accomplish a task even under the most stressful circumstances. Success breeds confidence. It's similar to when you're on a roll with the putter. Seems like the hole is as big as a basketball hoop.

The strategy of applying pressure on my opponent by hitting first into the green paid off in my first win as a pro.

BUILDING BLOCKS TO MENTAL TOUGHNESS

A player can become mentally tougher by learning from his experiences. The mind is like a computer with thousands of megabytes of memory. Store your experiences for when you will need them again because the game is a constant learning process. You should learn from your failures as well as successes. Ask yourself what you did or didn't do right in a situation. A lot of times you'll find it's the same thing over and over again.

■ Learn from your experiences, both positive and negative. Rallying to win three consecutive U.S. Juniors and as many U.S. Amateurs taught me the value of a never-give-up

attitude. Having lost a few leads, too, reinforced that attitude.

■ Take ownership of your mistakes. Every shot is your responsibility. When I drive it into the junk like I did on the last hole at Dubai in 2001, I can't blame anyone but myself. I hit the shot and I had to accept the consequences. It's not always easy, but it's fair.

■ Never make the same mistake twice. It took two visits to the tributary at Augusta National's 12th hole (in the 1999 and 2000 Masters) to convince me never to be short of that green again. Both times the wind got me, but that's no excuse. The wind is always a factor there.

■ Don't be afraid to turn a negative into a

positive. Someone once accused me of hitting into trouble so I could make an heroic recovery. They thought I got a rush out of it. They were only partly right. I would never intentionally hit into trouble, but I must admit to seeing opportunity where others might not. It's fun being able to hit a flop shot off a downhill lie within birdie range like I did on the eighth hole in the final round of the 2001 Masters. Again, I had hit it there and it was up to me to make the most of a dicey situation.

■ Never beat yourself up because there are plenty of people who will do it for you. I am my own worst critic, but I will never do anything to undermine my confidence. Nor will I be influenced by anyone's criticism or scrutiny of me. I was supposedly mired in a slump because I had gone six straight tournaments without a win at the start of the 2001 season. Well, we all know how that turned out. You have to be tough enough mentally to handle all potential distractions.

You can't miss nor can you wait to get to the next green. Your confidence builds with each putt you hole. Pretty soon you're on autopilot, playing by instinct and feel. That's as close to finding your own game as you can get. Sometimes we think too much instead of trusting that inner voice that says you can do it. We can think ourselves right into a bad swing or a costly mistake and our confidence suffers as a result. I know it's happened to me, although I must say when I was younger self-confidence was never an issue. Take my nature as an aggressive putter, for example. When I was a kid, I would knock a putt five feet past the hole and drain it coming back without even giving it a second thought. Only when I started thinking about the consequences of a miss did the hole begin to move on me, and too often I developed a case of "liprosy."

Intimidation is also difficult to put a finger on. How do you intimidate someone in a game where there is no physical contact? In football, if you have some guy 6-foot-5, 250 bearing down on you and you're 180 pounds soaking wet, that can be intimidating. But in golf intimidation is purely a state of mind rather than a fear of bodily harm. If you buy into the fact that you control your destiny, you'll never let another player impose his will on you or intimidate you. I also learned that very early in my career. I was an 11-year-old hotshot playing in the Junior World at Torrey Pines in San Diego. I had plenty of experience competing against guys much older and I didn't scare easily. My first-round opponent, however, was huge, about 6 feet, 180. Although he was only a year older, he could have been a defensive lineman on the varsity football team. To make matters worse, he was strong as a bull. His first drive took off like a rocket, eventually landing in the middle of the green of the par 4. I nearly freaked out. In fact, I was so intimidated I could barely breathe. I was not the same the rest of the week, barely speaking to my dad. On the way home, Pop asked me why I had been so quiet and I confessed being afraid. "Afraid of whom?" he asked. "The big kid," I said through a hard swallow. "Look, son," Pop said, "golf is played not by size but by skill, intelligence and guts." That's all he said, leaving me to chew on the words for a while. Great players like Gary Player and Teddy

I learned early that heart and talent can overcome a lack of physical stature.

Rhodes surely learned that lesson, too. I didn't know if I would ever grow big and strong, but I did know one thing: I'd never be intimidated by anyone or anything again.

Gamesmanship in golf is a lot more subtle than in other sports. Baseball great Babe Ruth would point to an area of the outfield where he intended the ball to exit the ballpark. Hall of Fame running back Jim Brown would drag himself up after a hard run as if he were taking his last breath, "unintentionally" stepping on a tackler in the process, then plow through the line with even more force on the next run. No one talked more trash than Michael Jordan and Larry Bird,

both superstars in a sport where cockiness and the ability to back it up on the court are accepted behavior. If you can get into your opponent's head and throw him off his game, that might be the edge you need in a close game or match.

I've had players pull a variety of things on me, from giving me a hard, cold stare after making a putt to hitting a certain club on a par 3 and suggesting to their caddie that they had hit another. I love the mind games. They're part of the fun of golf. I have mine, too. Here are my top 5. Feel free to try any or all of them.

■ Really lean on a drive, then react as if you mis-hit it.

■ On your way to a drive that you've nutted, take a quick look at your opponent's ball as you walk by, hesitate for a moment as if you think it's yours, then proceed to your drive.

■ Concede two or three short putts, then make your opponent putt a kick-in.

■ Make your opponent putt several gimmes, then concede a questionable two-footer.

■ After you've outdriven an opponent on a day marred by swirling winds, take a club you have no intention of hitting on your approach shot and make a few practice swings. If he's stealing your club selection, you might get him to guess wrong.

Guys like Freddie Couples and Ernie Els are so easygoing you'd never know from their demeanor what they're thinking. Others, like me, are more emotional and demonstrative. What we have in common is a competitive spirit that drives us to perform to the best of our abilities and an understanding that sometimes our best isn't good enough. Truth is we fail more often than we succeed. You can't let those failures get to you, because they will erode your confidence and chip away at your psyche. Pretty soon those inner demons will have you second-guessing everything from your swing to your putting stroke to the color of socks you're wearing.

I love the head-to-head competition and gamesmanship of match play. Sometimes the mind games are blatantly obvious; other times they're as subtle as nonchalance in the face of adversity.

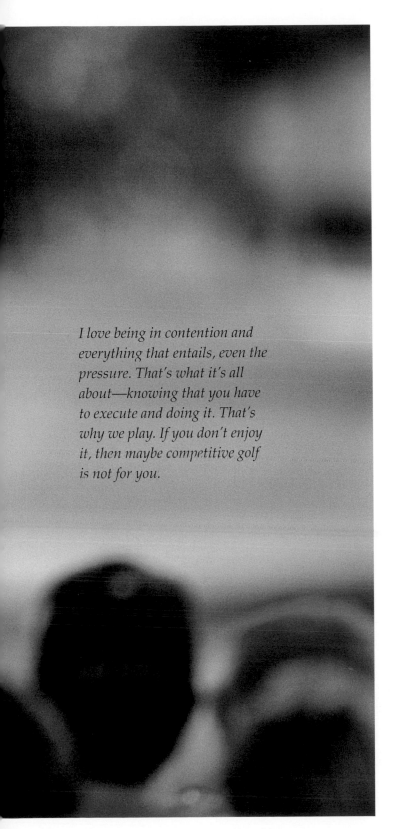

I love being in contention and everything that entails, even the pressure. That's what it's all about—knowing that you have to execute and doing it. That's why we play. If you don't enjoy it, then maybe competitive golf is not for you.

I personally have never experienced them, but I know some players who have not been as fortunate. The reason I've avoided those little devils is twofold. First, I refuse to give in to fear, real or imagined. I'm not talking about nervousness. I'm as nervous as the next guy every time I tee it up. Every competitor has a certain degree of anxiety. It goes with the territory. No, I'm referring to being afraid—either consciously or subconsciously—of anything or anyone. I've heard of players being afraid to win. Imagine that. When I turned pro, I took a lot of flak because I said my only purpose for playing was winning. I was only being honest. Second place still has no appeal for me. I would argue that most champions have that mindset. In order to be truly successful in any endeavor, you have to adopt a no-fear attitude. Don't be afraid to go for it.

Second, I refuse to yield to pressure. Some players wilt like lettuce when the heat is on. True competitors love the battle. Sure it gets intense and your nervous system is tested, but that's the most fun part of being a competitor. Ever wonder why Michael Jordan and Jack Nicklaus were so good in the clutch? Simple. They loved the spotlight and were inspired to reach another level of greatness by the need to accomplish. Give "M" the ball with the game on the line or Jack a must-make putt and watch them produce. That's because both of them had a winner's attitude to handling pressure: staying in their natural rhythm and routine, and focusing solely on what they needed to accomplish. "M" would bounce the ball a certain number of times at the foul line, spin the ball between his hands and fire away. Or he would beat a player off the dribble and never take his eyes off the basket until the ball had left his hands. And no one has ever concentrated on the task at hand better than Nicklaus. If you aspire to greatness, or if you're just seeking to get the most out of your ability, then you must be devoid of fear and oblivious to pressure.

LAY BACK IN MATCH PLAY

G olf is also a game of action and reaction. Knowing when and how to do either is a matter of experience. A lot of the strategy I employ when a medal-play tournament turns into match play is the result of past success and failure. I've learned when to be proactive. For example, sometimes I'll hit less club off the tee so I can hit first into the green and apply pressure on my opponent. The first time I used that strategy in a pro event was in a playoff against Davis Love III at the 1996 Las Vegas Invitational. Davis bombed a driver in perfect position on the first playoff hole. I followed with a 3-wood because I knew I could keep it in play with that club and hit short of his ball. Even though my approach was 20 feet right of the pin, he felt some pressure to get it inside me. He pulled his shot into the left bunker and made bogey. I two-putted for par and my first win as a pro. Recognizing when to be proactive and when to be reactive comes with experience and a feel for the situation.

Before an important shot, I relax myself by taking a long, deep breath.

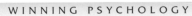

There is no better feeling than when a shot comes off exactly as you planned it. In order for that to happen consistently, though, you must commit totally to the shot you're trying to hit and trust your swing to deliver it. One without the other is a recipe for disaster.

A QUICK RECOVERY

I've hit a variety of snipes, quacks and shrimps in my lifetime, and if I continue to play I'll hit plenty more. I realize that a poor shot is just a swing away. I also realize that once I've hit a poor shot my only recourse is to hit a better shot on the next swing. In other words, I've learned how to hit it and forget it. There's no sense dwelling on a mistake. You can't hit the shot again, so forget about it. The same thing applies to my occasional emotional outbursts. They're no more than a release and once I get it out I'm fine. I realize that some of my comments, albeit self-directed, are X-rated and I apologize if they offend anyone. I wish I could vent without looking like a jerk. Unfortunately, I'm still working on it.

POWER OF POSITIVE THINKING

M y mom is one of those people who can find a silver lining in the darkest cloud. I guess I got my positive outlook from her, just as I got my relentless, never-ever-give-up attitude from my dad. Both require total belief in yourself and the ability to live with the outcome, whether good or bad. The road to failure is paved with negativity. If you think you can't do something, chances are you won't be able to. Conversely, the power of positive thinking can turn an adverse situation into a prime opportunity for heroism.

The final round of the 2001 Bay Hill Invitational is a perfect example. I took a one-shot lead into Sunday, but my swing abandoned me and with three holes to play I trailed Phil Mickelson by a shot. I managed to birdie the par-5 16th despite another errant tee shot, and my birdie putt at the par-3 17th singed the cup before sliding by. On the tough par-4 18th, I hit another snipe off the tee that hit a spectator. Fortunately, there was no injury. Even better, the deflection kept the ball from going out-of-bounds. Still I faced a shot of 192 yards into the green, the last few yards over water to a pin tucked back right. I was confident that if I trusted my swing—even though it had been shaky all day—I could pull off the shot. I hit a little cutter that settled about 15 feet from the hole. The sweeping putt (see the following pages) was center cut, too, and I won by one. Never did I let a negative thought enter my head. Never did I give up. Sometimes you look to be a hero; sometimes it finds you. Because I believe in myself, it has found me several times.

TIGER TALE:
CREATING THE WILL TO WIN

I'm asked all the time about my ability to focus and stay in the moment when the pressure is on. It's simple. I realize that the only thing I can control is my game. That is my only security blanket in a game where you could easily feel naked to the world. I can't count on controlling what the other

player is going to do because most top-level players are concentrating on their own games. Sometimes you win tournaments, other times they're given to you. The key is to consistently put yourself in position to win. That's the only way to get used to the pressure, so when you're faced with a must-make putt, you know the feelings that go along with it. More important, you know how to deal with them. Control yourself and you control your destiny. When I apply pressure on opponents it is a matter of controlling my game better than they do a shot at a time, moment by moment.

There is no sweeter feeling than knowing what I have to do to win, then calling on all my emotional control to pull it off, as I did here at Bay Hill in 2001.

FURTHER
THOUGHTS

❖ ❖ ❖

*Playing great golf is
much more than developing
solid fundamentals and sound
technique. It's about keeping
everything in perspective.*

•11•
HOW TO
GET STRONG

SURVIVING AS THE FITTEST

When I turned pro during the summer of 1996, I weighed 155 pounds in full golf gear. That's pretty light for 6-foot-2. I knew I had to get stronger and build up my entire body to endure the rigors of professional golf. I also wanted to add some shots to my arsenal that required strength. In addition, I knew that my body had not fully developed and that my swing would suffer as a result. It was particularly evident in my short irons. One minute I would hit a 9-iron 150 yards and the next 170. I needed to develop my muscles for consistency. The first couple of times I played in the Masters I had trouble hitting the green with a sand wedge in my hands. I would either blow it well over or suck the ball off those sloping surfaces. I remember being particularly frustrated by the ninth hole there during my debut in 1995. I hit what I thought was a perfect drive on No. 9 each round—well past the crosswalk—and twice my approach shot came rolling back down the hill to my feet because I hit it into the slope with too much juice. I would really go after a sand wedge in those days when I should have been hitting a little wedge and controlling the spin. Those little "arm" shots weren't available to me then because I wasn't strong enough to hit them. So one of the first things I did as a pro was alter my diet to increase my weight while limiting my body fat. I developed a physical fitness routine that would allow me to work every part of my body. I wanted to have effortless power and the ability to hit little finesse scoring shots. And when I really had to lean on one, I wanted to be able to do so without losing my balance. In order to accomplish my goals I had to get stronger.

I've always been into physical fitness, so it was just a matter of refining my workout to include stretching, aerobics and weight training. My intention was to work every muscle so I would not only increase my strength but my endurance, too. I don't know how much stretching Sam Snead does, but I'm told he is one of the most flexible athletes ever. He could kick the top of an eight-foot ceiling when he was 75 years old. Sam could also touch his left thumb against his left forearm without help from his other hand. Even more amazing was the sight of Sam bending over and picking his ball out of the cup without bending his knees. Talk about flexible, the man was like a rubber band. I'm sure that's a big reason for his longevity in a sport where the longer you play the shorter your back-swing gets. That's because the muscles in the upper body lose their elasticity through the aging process and restrict the shoulder turn. Sam is living proof that you can minimize the effects of time by remaining flexible.

I learned the value of staying in shape as a youth running cross-country. I also learned that the harder you run, the quicker it's over. That's why I run as fast as I can for three to five miles whenever the weather and my schedule allow it. When they don't, the stationary bicycle is a nice option. When I first started on the bike, I had to set it at almost a beginner's level. Even then my legs felt like they were going to fall off after only a few minutes. My stamina increased gradually. Now I can ride that baby at nearly the maximum

level of difficulty until I'm ready to quit. That's how you should approach each part of your workout—with caution. Build your routine slowly to avoid injury and maximize the benefits. At the conclusion of your run take 10 or 15 minutes to cool off before beginning the rest of your workout. During this time completely clear your mind of all thoughts. Train yourself to think of nothing at all. You'll be surprised how refreshed you feel afterward. It's also effective when you run into a traffic jam on the golf course. Clearing your mind for even a few minutes will sharpen your focus when you really need it.

Sam Snead was so flexible, he could kick a ceiling, well into his 70s.

12 Keys to Healthy Running:

■ I dress appropriately for the weather; light clothing in warm weather, layered in cold weather.

■ I find a comfortable pair of running shoes; and I change them before they wear out.

■ I wear a wool cap in cold weather.

■ I always stretch before I run.

■ I avoid running during the heat of the day.

■ I never run on a full stomach.

■ I drink plenty of water before I run.

■ I maintain a steady pace.

The behind-the-back stretch helps me prevent injury.

HOW I KEEP MY MUSCLES LIMBER

· ·

Here are several stretching exercises to help keep your golf muscles supple. Do them gently at first, and if you feel pain scale back. You should check with your doctor before beginning any new exercise or fitness routine:

My fitness routine allows me to be this flexible in my neck and shoulders.

■ *Lower Back:* From a standing position, bend from the waist and try to touch your toes; hold for 20 seconds; repeat as many times as you wish. From a sitting position, bend from the waist and try to touch the floor between your feet; hold for 10 seconds; repeat as many times as you wish. Often during my warm-up, I will take a club and hold it across my upper back and shoulders parallel to the ground. From that position I'll slowly make shoulder turns back and forth to stretch out the back muscles and loosen up.

■ *Hips:* Lie on your back with your legs extended; lock your hands under your knee and pull your leg toward your chest while keeping your other leg extended; hold for 20 seconds; repeat with your other leg.

■ *Chest:* From a standing position, lock your hands behind your back and raise them while fully expanding your chest; hold for 20 seconds; repeat as many times as you wish.

■ *Shoulders:* From a standing position, extend your left arm over your shoulder behind your back and try to grab your right hand, which you have reached under your shoulder and behind your back; hold for 20 seconds; reverse arms and repeat. At first you might not be able to touch your fingers but as the muscles stretch you should be able to give yourself a low-five behind your back.

■ *Hamstrings ("Hammies"):* From a sitting position, spread your legs as far apart as possible; try to grab your left foot with both hands while keeping your legs extended; hold for 20 seconds; repeat with your right foot.

■ *Hands and Fingers:* A lot of players don't realize the importance of flexibility in your hands. Shake your hands for a few minutes like a swimmer does before competition. It will help you develop soft hands for those touch shots around the green.

I never sit on a tee unless it's a long wait.

- I include hilly terrain in my course.
- I cool off for 10 to 15 minutes before resuming my workout.
- I drink plenty of water afterward.
- I always stretch after I run.

I believe great physical conditioning gives me an advantage when I have to play 36 holes in a match-play event like the U.S. Amateur or the Ryder Cup, or when the weather has forced a postponement. It gives me an extra gear when I need it. I needed it during the final round of the 2000 NEC Invitational in Akron, Ohio, a real marathon because of a weather delay. We finished that tournament in near darkness, and I felt just as fresh in the end as during my warm-up that morning. Fatigue can affect your focus and cause you to make a bad decision. I never want to

lose a tournament because of a bad decision precipitated by my being out of shape. In Akron, being at my physical best helped me stay mentally sharp and allowed me to claim another trophy.

As an international player I have traveled through half a dozen time zones in 24 hours, and

Since the muscles can get a little tight during delays, I make it a practice to stretch a bit to maintain some elasticity. I can't turn my shoulders to their fullest extent if my neck muscles are tight.

Because I compete around the world, my fitness regimen is key.

*Even at the end of a grueling
72 holes, I often feel energized.*

I believe being aerobically fit helps my body recover quickly so that I'm able to compete at the highest level. My road trips take me to Bangkok one day and St. Andrews the next, but being physically ready to play should still be a priority. Remember your cardiovascular system and it will pay off in the long run.

Weight training is exactly that—training your muscles through the use of free weights or an exercise machine. I believe it is necessary for a player to maximize his power and control. That's why I train every muscle, among them tris (triceps), bis (biceps), quads (quadriceps), pects (pectorals) and abs (abdominals). I do curls for girls and also to build some powerful bis.

Any workout routine must be regimented and consistent. You can't lift weights this week and not the next. It requires a real commitment to building a powerful body, toning it or whatever your overall goal might be. I lift three to five times a week. My preround routine is dictated by my tee time. For example, I might eliminate weight lifting and concentrate more on the rest of my workout for an early tee time. The key is to be loose, fluid and in my natural rhythm prior to and during a round. I use different amounts of weight for different parts of my body, and I vary my reps. Of course, the heaviest weight is reserved for my legs, which are the strongest part of my body.

I like to work with free weights because I can set my body in different angles and positions to work on different moves, plus they provide more range of movement. I can also work on my stabilization muscles in particular areas better, but occasionally I'll use a machine when free weights aren't available. To avoid pulling a muscle or straining myself, I always stretch before lifting and I never do heavy lifting without a spotter. Most physical fitness experts recommend working

MY BEST STRENGTH EXERCISES FOR GOLF

• • • • • • • • • • • • • • • • • • •

The upper body is your swing's engine. You have to keep it fine-tuned to maximize performance. I want mine operating on all cylinders in the heat of competition. Here are some recommended exercises to strengthen your upper back, shoulders, chest, arms and abs:

■ Lat (latissimus dorsi) pulldowns for the upper back.
■ Seated rows (a rowing motion from a seated position) for rotator cuffs.
■ Overhead press for shoulders.
■ Horizontal bench press, incline bench press and some type of fly for the chest. The last is a favorite of body builders and one that you should work your way up to. The exercise requires you to lie flat on a bench with dumbbells in each hand. Hold the dumbbells palms down, parallel to the bench. Extend them away from your body and, in an arcing motion, bring them up until your hands touch above your chest. You must keep your elbows slightly bent. Don't lock them.
■ Pushdowns, dips or overhead tricep extensions (any combination) for the triceps.
■ Horizontal and vertical wrist curls for the forearms.
■ Standard stomach crunch—you can do them anywhere—and knee lifts up to your chest for the abs.

Just as form is an important element of the golf swing, it is also an important factor in weight training. Always maintain good form to get the desired results. Remember to start out moderately and exercise caution. Don't take on more than you can handle. Building up your muscle strength while you're young will help you maintain it as you get older. A healthy body and a more powerful swing that lasts a lifetime will be your ultimate reward.

HOW I USE A WEIGHTED CLUB

Increasing and maintaining flexibility in my muscles has had a positive impact on my overall performance and has helped me avoid injury. It is a major part of my physical fitness program, which consists of a total body workout of about one to two hours, three to five times a week, depending upon my schedule. I also recommend the use of a weighted golf club without a ball to assist in warming up before a practice session. It is great for stretching out those upper-body muscles, but you must swing it slowly. If swung properly, a weighted club can also increase your swing speed.

■ I loosen up first; I warm up my muscles.

■ I start each swing from the address position.

■ Easy does it; I swing the club slowly and deliberately to avoid pulling a muscle.

■ I swing the club, I don't let the club swing me, because its momentum can pull me all over the place if I'm not careful.

■ I maintain my body positions, especially my spine angle.

different body parts on different days. For example, you might concentrate on your upper body today, legs and lower body tomorrow, then upper body again the next day. Or you might lift every other day. Variety can keep your routine from becoming monotonous and make it more fun than work. You might also consider mixing a light cardio day with a heavy lifting one. You must customize your routine according to what works best for you. Again, I would caution you to get a complete physical examination before undertaking any strenuous exercise regimen. Make no mistake, weight training

not only works the muscles but the heart, too.

Since legs provide the foundation for a golf swing, I would recommend the following exercises to help you build a solid base: extensions, curls, presses, plus regular squats or hack squats. The last are probably the single most important exercise for building strong legs. They really work the quads, hamstrings, buttocks, lower back and gluteus maximus. It's also a terrific exercise for developing overall stamina and strength. You have to be very careful with squats, though. It's easy to pull a muscle, so try not to overdo it. For the

My training program has helped me develop my upper body.

NUTRITION: MY WINNING DIET

Ten to Win

Foods that are high in nutrition but low in fat.

- Any vegetable or fruit that is orange in color—cantaloupe, sweet potato, squash and carrots
- Most green vegetables and fruits
- Turkey
- Whole grains
- Baked/broiled fish
- Baked/grilled chicken
- Skim milk
- Egg whites
- Rice
- Fruit juices

Ten to Lose

Food loaded with empty calories.

- Pizza
- Ice cream
- Cheese cake
- Roast beef/prime rib
- Fried chicken
- Fried fish
- Gravy
- Potato chips
- Ham
- Soft drinks

TEN TO LOSE

average person seeking to build and maintain muscle strength, I recommend two sets for each exercise; the first set of 10 to 12 reps at a weight that doesn't exhaust you. For the second set, I'd increase the weight by 15 to 20 percent, which should increase the difficulty about the same amount. For example, you might only be able to complete seven or eight reps of the second set. That burning sensation in your muscles is a sign that you're getting the best results from your workout.

Changing my eating habits was the hard part. It meant cutting back on my two favorite food groups—fast foods (cheeseburgers, fries and strawberry milkshakes) and faster foods (pizza, hot wings and tacos). When I became of age, I also liked to share a beer or two with friends. I quickly learned that in order to increase my strength through muscle I had to avoid grease and cut out all empty calories (non-nutritional foods; anything cooked in oil or fat).

Good nutrition, including drinking plenty of water, is fundamental to my success under trying conditions, such as excessive heat and humidity.

I'm about a buck 80 (180 pounds) and my percentage of body fat is a bogey on a par 4, so while there is still room for improvement I've done a decent job of putting on the right kind of weight. But more importantly, my energy level and stamina are the highest since I was a kid. I attribute it to watching what and when I eat.

I can't plan your diet for you because everyone is different. What works for me might not work for you. There are, however, some foods that are not conducive to good health. I recommend that you minimize your amount

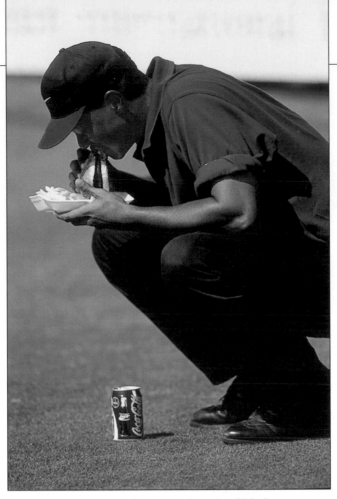

Gone are the days when I gobbled down a hamburger and fries at the turn.

- Sport drinks can help me avoid dehydration.
- Fruits are a good source of energy, namely apples and bananas.
- I avoid sugar highs from chocolate during a round.
- I avoid heavy food (hamburgers, hotdogs, etc.) at the halfway house; they can make me lethargic.
- I avoid late meals; I give my food time to digest before I lie down.
- Most desserts are deadly; I substitute fruits and frozen yogurt.

of dairy fat like cheese, cream and whole milk products and pick leaner cuts of meat. You don't have to become a vegetarian. I'm not. In fact, I still have a cheeseburger every once in a while, but I never pig out on them. I pick my spots. The key is moderation. Find out what works best for you and stick with it. Your physical fitness routine will be more effective if you follow a balanced diet.

My Dietary Do's and Don'ts
- I avoid teeing off on a full stomach; I eat at least two hours before my tee time to give my food time to digest.
- I drink plenty of water before and during the round.
- I keep a good supply of nutrition bars in my bag for instant energy.

I've tried to limit my salt and sugar intake, but I'm still a sucker for Mom's sticky rice and mangoes. Good thing she doesn't make it too often. You need a little bit of fat to maintain your weight. Just don't get carried away.

I've already admitted being a fast-food junkie when I was younger. I remember Pop's lecture about the evils of fast food. "Son," he said, "enjoy your youth but you know those foods are not healthy for you. Someday you'll decide on your own to eat healthier." He said it was my responsibility and that he didn't want to deny me the kind of pleasure a kid derives from a Big Mac, fries and a shake. Boy, was I glad to hear that. "But with age comes responsibility," Pop said. "I know you'll take the responsibility for your own health when that day comes." That's all he said. Pop was right. That day came sooner than I thought, and I'm much the better for it. You will be, too.

SOME OF MY SHOTS
REQUIRE SPECIFIC STRENGTH

· ·

A lot of what I've been able to accomplish in golf is the direct result of becoming physically stronger. I couldn't play shots like the 2-iron "stinger" two or three years ago because I didn't have the strength in my wrists and forearms to execute them. I had to make my body complement my mind to make the most of my natural ability. In this game you need every edge, and physical strength has definitely become one of mine.

12

HOW TO PLAY

ENJOYING THE JOURNEY

I don't know the exact percentage, but a great number of novice golfers find the game too difficult, get frustrated, quit and never touch another golf club. I also know of some very good players who experienced success in the game but somewhere along the journey lost their zeal for it and walked away. I believe they lost sight of the reason they fell in love with the game in the first place. Golf hooked them not because they were good at it but because they derived great pleasure from it. I played several sports as a youth. I also ran cross-country and really enjoyed it. But golf was the most fun. It still is.

I mentioned earlier that golf was like a childhood friend. While other kids were stuck inside on bad-weather days in a state of boredom, I was being entertained by golf. I turned our living room into a chipping area. I would hit flop shots off the carpet over the coffee table and land the ball short of the fireplace. I never broke anything although I came close a few times. People are always asking me about the pressure of tournament golf. I'll let you in on a little secret. I had to hit those floppers so they made little or no noise because if Mom had heard me hitting balls in her living room, she would have blistered my behind. The pressure of tournament golf pales in comparison.

During the summer, Pop would drop me off at Heartwell Golf Course on his way to work, and I would spend all day on my playground. I would arrive about 9 A.M. and go straight to the practice range. I'd play nine holes, take a lunch break, then play nine more. Then I would work on my short game until Pop picked me up. Every once in a while Stuart Reed, a member of the European PGA Tour who lived in Long Beach, would come to Heartwell for a practice session. Stuart and I became fast friends. We would have so much fun practicing, trying to outdo each other. I was only 5 or 6 and no way could I match his long game, but I gave him a run for his money on short shots. We would create situations like trying to putt the ball directly behind a light pole or lobbing it into a trash can. The fun part was creating shots to escape obstacles. Sometimes Stuart would show me how; other times I'd discover it myself. Golf has always been a game to me.

The most fun I ever had, though, was playing with my dad. The competition got pretty fierce at times, too. He established par for me based on how many strokes it would take me to reach a green under normal conditions, plus two putts. For example, on a natural par 4 that took me four shots to get to the green, because I couldn't hit it that far as a kid, my par would be 6. We also played all kinds of shotmaker games. For example, Pop would pick out a target and we would see who could hit it closer to that target. The trick was you couldn't hit it straight at the target. You had to either cut the ball or hook it and vary the trajectory. And you had to call it in advance. Some of the shots you see me hit in competition today were dug out of the dirt of a practice range in shotmaker games with Pop. We would always laugh, share a hug and a soft drink afterward. Well, I'd have a Cherry Coke; Pop's choice was a little stronger.

The game should never be boring, especially when you're working to improve. I have just as much fun on the practice range and green as on the golf course. I love working on shots, carving them this way and that, and proving to myself that I can hit a certain shot on command. You can build a lot of confidence in your game and have fun doing it by trying these games during practice:

Different Club, Same Distance—With the exception of the first few wedges that I hit to warm up, I always hit to a target. So, use the 150-yard marker as your target. Start with your 150-yard club (for me it's a hard 9-iron) and work up to your 2-iron hitting balls to the target. This is a great drill for controlling distance by controlling arm speed.

9-Ball—Pick a spot about five yards off the chipping green. Use nine balls, three each for three

I try to keep my life in perspective, remembering to sit back and relax. Trick-shot artist Dennis Walters, and his dog, Benji Hogan, perform at many of my clinics. We have a great time together.

Here, at one of my junior clinics, I am trying hard to be a trick-shot artist.

different clubs, the lob wedge, pitching wedge and 8-iron (I'll sometimes substitute my 3-wood). Hit to the hole farthest from the spot. See how many shots you can get up and down with each club. Keep score. You'll be surprised how quickly your feel around the green will improve. I play a similar putting game using driver, sand wedge and 2-iron. It's great for helping ingrain the feeling of releasing the putterhead.

Putt and Pull Back—You'll need a partner for this game. The two of you must putt from the same dis-

tance. Whoever is farthest from the hole afterward must increase that distance by a putterlength. The objective is to hole out in the least number of strokes. The winner selects the starting point for the next hole. There is not a better drill for lag putting, especially if you have lunch riding on the outcome.

Flop It—I wouldn't suggest hitting flop shots in your living room like I did, but you can get similar results by using your shag bag. Place it or a bucket or a towel about 15 yards away and see how many balls you can flop into it with your lob wedge.

Someone played a trick on me and substituted a powder ball. We all got a good laugh.

H-O-R-S-E—It's played just like the basketball game. Toss a coin or a tee to see who goes first. That player selects a spot from which to putt and keeps honors as long as that player makes the putt. The second player must answer. That player gets a letter for every missed putt. Whoever spells horse first loses.

My friends and I always have some kind of competition going during practice unless we're preparing for a major championship. Then we concentrate on the task at hand. We always find a way to make the game fair and fun. One of my favorites is played like strip poker in reverse. It's a team match. The team that wins the hole loses a club of the other team's choice from the winning team's bag. It's the only game I've played where the winner actually loses. Here are some other games sure to keep things interesting:

Wolf/Pig—Ideally this game is played by a foursome. By coin toss or tee toss, a player is selected "wolf" on the first tee. That designation changes on successive holes so that each player has been on each hole for low total. If a team gets all six points on a hole, that total is doubled and the umbrella goes up. It's like the white towel being waved by the losers.

Vegas—You need an accurate scorekeeper for this one, because every player's score is used on each hole. The low score between partners is put first. For example, if I make a 4 and my partner makes a 6 our score is 46. If our opponents score 45, they get one point on the hole. If a team makes birdie, the other team has to reverse its score. For example, if the other team scores 47, it would be 74 as the result of my team's birdie. If both teams birdie, then both scores are reversed and the difference awarded the team with the lowest score.

You might find this hard to believe but even when I'm grinding on the final nine of a tournament, I'm having a blast. Admittedly, some players are more demonstrative with their enthusiasm. Lee Trevino interacts with playing partners and the gallery. Chi Chi Rodriguez entertains. Arnold Palmer says more with a smile than with a thousand words. I believe even the most stoic player is having the time of his life when the game is on. If he isn't he shouldn't be playing.

Part of my competitive pleasure is pushing myself to the limit. It is an inner conflict with which every competitor can identify. Sometimes I surprise myself. When I won the Masters for the second time to hold all four professional major titles simultaneously, I was amazed at how I was able to get my game to peak four times within a year exactly as I had worked so hard to do. The competition down the stretch at Augusta National

I'm not a comedian, but I've been known to crack a joke to relieve tension during competition.

the wolf four times through the 16th hole. The wolf has the option of choosing a partner after the tee shots or playing the other three on his own. The selected player can deny the partnership, taking on the other three himself, thus becoming a "pig." Points are accrued on each hole. The player with the least amount of points loses to everyone.

Umbrella—This is a six-point game played among partners. Single points are awarded on each hole for low ball, closest to the pin and birdie. If a team has the high score on a hole, it must surrender a point to the other team. Two points are awarded

was fierce and unforgettable. David Duval was making a run. Phil Mickelson was right there and I managed to make a putt or two. If that kind of competition doesn't get your juices flowing, nothing will. I was fortunate to get some breaks and win, but everyone was a winner that day.

There is no greater joy in this game than being able to give back. I love working with kids, helping

Whether I'm playing or working, I think it's smart to sit back and relax. It's a philosophy that has served me well so far.

them achieve their dreams, whether in golf or life. I owe a debt of gratitude to a lot of people who helped me attain my dreams, and I'm determined to help others. I take my responsibility as a role model very seriously. By positively influencing others, I believe I can make a difference. The smiles on the faces of kids grateful to get a few minutes of instruction warm my heart. I am grateful to golf for giving me that feeling. In the big picture what truly matters is the lives we touch. That is how we measure our legacy. I measure mine in the warmth of those smiles.

My parents have been the biggest influence in my life. They taught me to give of myself, my time, talent, and, most of all, my love. I have never forgotten those early lessons of life. I hope you won't forget the lessons you've learned from the pages of this book.

I love this game because it has loved me. I love it because it has allowed me to give you the best of me. And that is the most fun of all.

I welcome my responsibility as a role model for kids. If I can make a positive impact, I am happy.

*If you're not having fun playing this great game, do something to
change your perspective. Having fun leads to great golf and vice versa.
And don't forget to take time to smell the roses along the way.*

AFTERWORD

The 1996 U.S. Amateur at Pumpkin Ridge relates to the way a golfer intent on improving should approach this book. I had just busted a big drive on the par-4 16th hole in my second-round match against Jerry Courville, a very good player from Connecticut. When I got to my ball, I found it had settled into the first cut of rough, about one foot off the fairway. Amid dead silence, I was about to pull a club from my bag when a familiar voice rang out from 50 yards away.

"You can't count that as a fairway hit in regulation!"

I looked across the fairway and there was my dad, standing under a tree, smiling. Leave it to Pop to yell something like that while I was trying to win a tournament, which at that point was the most important one of my life, going for my third Amateur in a row. It was so much like him, I just shook my head and laughed. Pop's calling attention to a detail like that was indicative of the way he raised me. He didn't believe in cutting corners, not in golf or anything else. His approach to achieving a goal was to formulate a game plan and proceed systematically. Along the way, you assessed and reassessed your strengths and weaknesses honestly—if a ball stopped one inch off the fairway, you didn't count it as a fairway hit. That philosophy is the best way to get the most out of this book. Now that you've read it once, read it again. Spend a bit more time on each section and concentrate on mastering the individual points I've laid out for you. Practice them. Think about them. Don't move ahead until you're able to perform each movement to your satisfaction. It takes some time and effort, but it's worth it. What at first appears to be drudgery in golf, turns out to be extremely interesting, fun and rewarding. I love walking onto the practice range with the specific goal of ironing out some swing problem. I'm never intimidated by the problem, though I do get frustrated sometimes trying to solve it. I know the answer is out there.

I hope this book has helped your game already. Passing my knowledge on to you has been a great pleasure and a privilege.

—TIGER WOODS, *Autumn 2001*